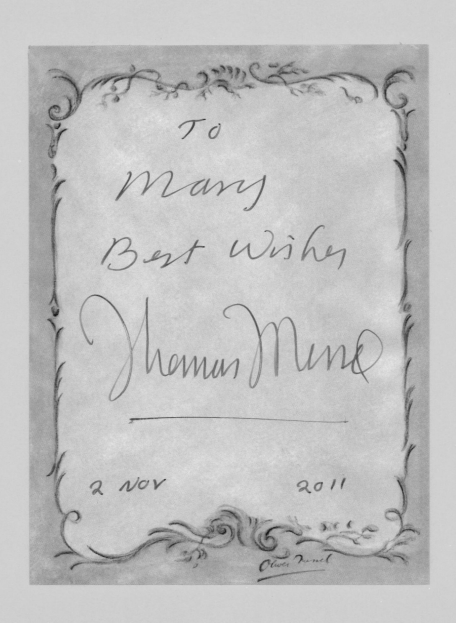

To
Mary
Best Wishes
Thomas Mink

2 NOV   2011

Oliver Mink

OLIVER MESSEL

In the Theatre of Design

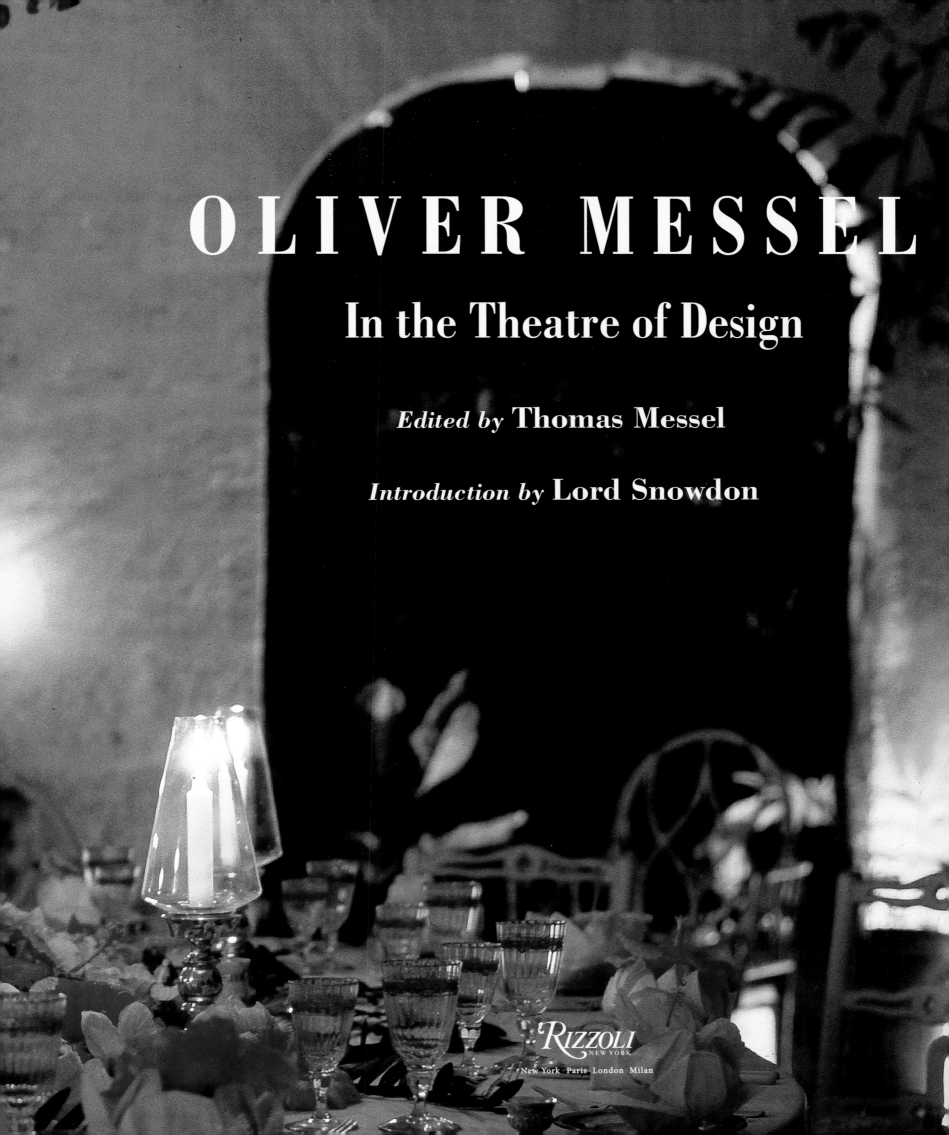

OLIVER MESSEL

In the Theatre of Design

Edited by **Thomas Messel**

Introduction by **Lord Snowdon**

RIZZOLI
NEW YORK

New York · Paris · London · Milan

PAGE 1 *Messel's 1961 designs for the restoration of the ballroom at the Bath Assembly Rooms.*

PAGES 2-3 *Maddox, Messel's home on Barbados.*

PAGES 4-5 *The drawing room of the Dorchester Hotel's Oliver Messel suite.*

To the life and work of my beloved uncle Oliver Messel.

Contents

Acknowledgments

First and foremost my thanks are to Pepe, my beloved wife, who has shared this book with me from the start and who, as an artist, guided me with her aesthetic and sensitive eye.

I owe a great debt of thanks to Helen Fry, who as my right hand, with consummate skill and technical expertise, has made this book possible, and to Fran Costello, who has latterly shared this enterprise.

I wish to thank Joe Cicio for suggesting that I produce this book, Susanne Earls Carr in supporting the project with Rizzoli, and Sally Chichester for her publishing expertise and for directing me through every step.

One of the many joys that I have experienced throughout this enterprise is the genuine enthusiasm and generosity of spirit it has engendered in everyone I have encountered. My gratitude to them is immense, most particularly the writers, Sarah Woodcock, Stephen Calloway, Jeremy Musson, and Keith Lodwick, as well as the photographer Nic Barlow. I have been generously supported by personal contributions from Tony Snowdon, Carolina Herrera, Sir Roy Strong, Desmond Heeley, Nicky Haslam, Hamish Bowles, Sir Kenneth Adam, Sir Christopher Frayling, and Anthony Powell, whose comments have enriched this book.

Very special thanks to my cousins Tony and Lucy Snowdon for their encouragement and to Lynne Wilson for coordinating the use of the Snowdon photographs and image rights. Also, my thanks to Derry Moore for his generosity in allowing the use of his photographs.

David Morton and Charles Miers of Rizzoli in New York had the faith and vision to realize the idea and quality of this book right from the start. I am also indebted to Abigail Sturges for her picture editing and layout and to Ron Broadhurst for his supervision and editing of the script.

Central to this book has been the involvement of the Victoria and Albert Museum, Department of Theatre and Performance, who have been more than generous over the past five years, especially Director Geoffrey Marsh and Dr. James Fowler, who have been truly enthusiastic allies, and Mark Eastment, Director of V&A Publications.

My profound gratitude goes to many members of Oliver's family and friends for access to their artwork, letters, and recollections, particularly to William (Earl of) Rosse, David (Viscount) Linley, Polly Jeremy and Linley Lewis, Reinaldo Herrera, Tom (Viscount) De Vesci, and Tommy Baptiste.

The National Trust at Nymans, in particular Rebecca Graham and Jean Taylor, provided generous access to their archives and research. Clarinda Chan and Reena Suleman of The Royal Borough of Kensington and Chelsea supplied images of Linley Sambourne House. My thanks to Ralph Adron for his Oliver Messel paint recipe, and to Beth Daugherty for her wise introductions to the principles of designing such a book as this.

Along with Sarah Woodcock and Keith Lodwick, I would like to express our thanks to their colleagues at the V&A Department of Theatre and Performance, especially to Dr. Janet Birkett, Donald Darroch, Dr. Kate Dorney, Cathy Haill, Dr. Beverley Hart, Claire Hudson, Amy King, Andrew Kirk, Jane Pritchard, Kirstian Volsing, and Thea Stevenson. Also to Francesca Franchi and David Ogden of the Royal Opera House archives department for the access and use of their images.

I would like to share my thanks, with Jeremy Musson, to Rosanna Crawley of the Dorchester Hotel; Philip and Tonya Watkins and Lynn Zijlmans of Flaxley Abbey; Hew Blaire of Justerini and Brooks; Nick Rayne of Rayne-Delman; Lord Farringdon and David Freeman, curator of Buscot Park; Lady Emma Barnard and Richard Pailthorpe, curator of Parham; and Julia Ayres, archivist of Glyndebourne. My thanks to Mathew Claridge for images of his and his father Johnny Claridge's restorations at the Dorchester Hotel and to Richard Elder, director of Rosehill Theatre. Further thanks also to Timothy Morgan-Owen, Peter Rice, Pat Albeck, Sir Arthur Bryan of Wedgewood, and Andrea Tanner, archivist at Fortnum and Mason.

I am exceptionally grateful to William and Usha Gordon for their kindness and hospitality in enabling Jeremy to travel and stay with them at Fustic House on Barbados, and to The Mustique Land Company, with the Hon. Brian Alexander, Jeanette Cadet, Pippa Williamson, Mr. Straker, and Debbie Charles, for arranging his visit and comprehensive tour of all the Messel houses on Mustique and for access and use of their photographic images. Special thanks to Joan Carlisle-Irving for her hospitality at Sea Star, and to Nick Parravicino for organizing his schedule on Barbados, with further thanks to Robert Thompson, Jenny Hall, Lucia Graves, Sam Mahon, Patricia Forde, Larry Warren, Sir Anthony and Lady Bamford, Bryan Adams, the Countess of Litchfield, David Whelan, Mr. and Mrs. Anthony Johnson, the Hon. David Bernstein, and the late Lord Glenconner.

Thanks to David Robertson, Lauretta Dives, and Phil Moad at Kobal Picture Desk and to Ann Golding of Camera Press.

On behalf of all the writers, I would like also to thank members of the V&A Photo Studio: Santiago Arribas, Ellie Atkins, Pip Barnard, Henrietta Clare, Clare Johnson, Ken Jackson, and James Stevenson. Many thanks also to David Robertson.

During the five years that this book has taken to complete I have been overwhelmed by the generous response of so many people who have been inspired by Oliver and do hope that I have made no omissions of gratitude in this acknowledgment.

The Messel Family Tree

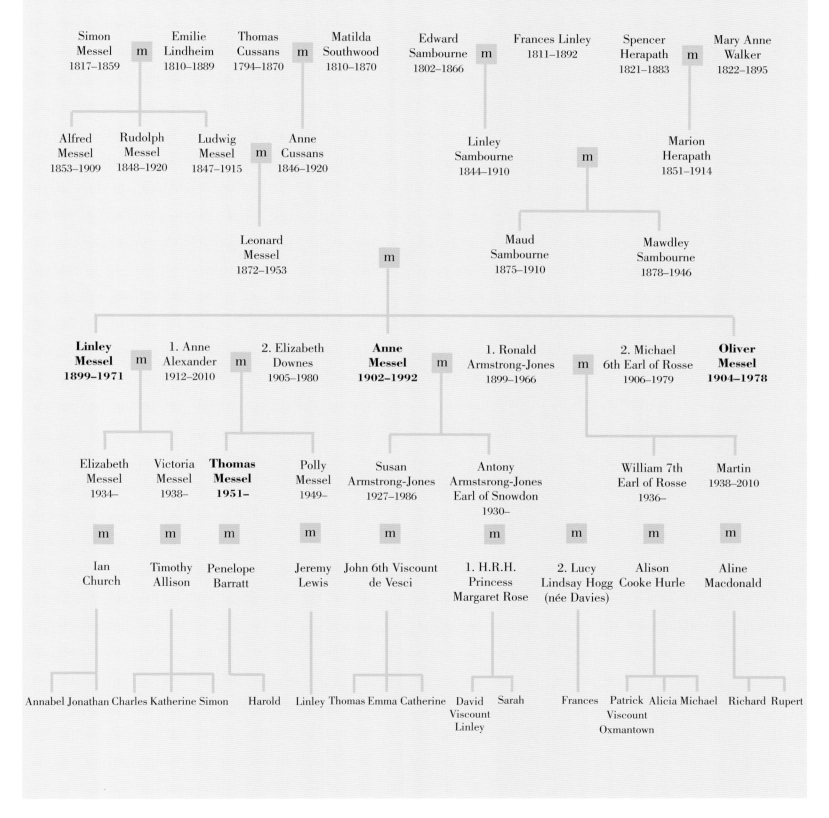

Simon Messel 1817–1859 **m** Emilie Lindheim 1810–1889

Thomas Cussans 1794–1870 **m** Matilda Southwood 1810–1870

Edward Sambourne 1802–1866 **m** Frances Linley 1811–1892

Spencer Herapath 1821–1883 **m** Mary Anne Walker 1822–1895

Alfred Messel 1853–1909

Rudolph Messel 1848–1920

Ludwig Messel 1847–1915 **m** Anne Cussans 1846–1920

Linley Sambourne 1844–1910 **m** Marion Herapath 1851–1914

Leonard Messel 1872–1953 **m**

Maud Sambourne 1875–1910

Mawdley Sambourne 1878–1946

Linley Messel 1899–1971 **m** 1. Anne Alexander 1912–2010 **m** 2. Elizabeth Downes 1905–1980

Anne Messel 1902–1992 **m** 1. Ronald Armstrong-Jones 1899–1966 **m** 2. Michael 6th Earl of Rosse 1906–1979

Oliver Messel 1904–1978

Elizabeth Messel 1934–

Victoria Messel 1938–

Thomas Messel 1951–

Polly Messel 1949–

Susan Armstrong-Jones 1927–1986

Antony Armstrong-Jones Earl of Snowdon 1930–

William 7th Earl of Rosse 1936–

Martin 1938–2010

m **m** **m** **m** **m** **m** **m** **m** **m**

Ian Church

Timothy Allison

Penelope Barratt

Jeremy Lewis

John 6th Viscount de Vesci

1. H.R.H. Princess Margaret Rose

2. Lucy Lindsay Hogg (née Davies)

Alison Cooke Hurle

Aline Macdonald

Annabel Jonathan Charles Katherine Simon Harold Linley Thomas Emma Catherine David Viscount Linley Sarah Frances Patrick Viscount Oxmantown Alicia Michael Richard Rupert

7

Foreword

by Tony Snowdon

Oliver, photographed by his nephew Antony Armstrong-Jones (Earl of Snowdon) while staying as Oliver's guest in Venice, 1956.

My uncle, Oliver Messel, was a very strong influence on my life and work. When I was six, he let me help him make some masks in his studio for a Cochran revue. Later I went with him on my first visit to Venice, where he taught me to use my eyes.

He was unquestionably the outstanding theatre designer of his day. In 1932, his white-on-white set for Cochran's *Helen!* got a standing ovation every night: it had an enormous influence on interior decorators of the 1930s. He developed his own kind of romantic baroque with productions at Covent Garden and his costume and sets for Glyndebourne, which were what everybody longed for after the austerity of the war. He had a flawless sense of colour; but he will perhaps be best remembered for his own original form of romanticism in the stage productions of *Ring Round the Moon* and *House of Flowers*.

Oliver was a master of illusion and make-believe; often you'd find that he'd personally made a chandelier with sticky paper and fuse wire, or constructed the dancers' headdresses out of pipe cleaners. When I was a child, I found a bird's nest in his London garden; on inspection I discovered it was made by him, and the eggs were hand-painted china.

He was extremely practical, making all his own models, down to the last detail. He had the respect of everyone in the theatre because he knew which way the fabric was cut and how every prop could be made. He would work all night. He had endless energy and was very strong willed, in fact, a perfectionist.

Chapter 1

My Uncle Oliver
A Private View

by Thomas Messel

OPPOSITE *Oliver's matinee-idol looks are captured in this Clarence Sinclair Bull portrait of 1936 taken in Hollywood while he was working on the MGM film* Romeo and Juliet.

Oliver Messel was the preeminent British stage designer and decorator for much of the twentieth century. His work was characterized by his own innate sense of romance, charm, and wit, and his remarkable talents extended beyond the stage to encompass painting, interior design, architecture, and film. To me Oliver was my adored uncle, the younger brother of my father, Linley. From the age of twenty in the late 1960s and through the 1970s I grew to know Oliver extremely well. As Oliver wrote to me, "Had you been my own son, there might have been that parental generation barrier, whereas as it is, as you grow up, it has been such a joy to discover that you care about, and are interested in all the things that mean everything to me and that we can laugh together at the same things, as it were on the same wavelength, which means friendship, not just a relation."

Oliver made his first appearance in the early hours of 13 January 1904 and was raised at 104 Lancaster Gate, the imposing white stuccoed London home of Leonard and Maud Messel, overlooking Hyde Park, where he joined older siblings Linley (born 1899) and Anne (born 1902). That this child should be artistic was almost preordained, arriving as he did at the confluence of a heritage of artistic talent.

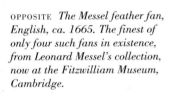

OPPOSITE *The Messel feather fan, English, ca. 1665. The finest of only four such fans in existence, from Leonard Messel's collection, now at the Fitzwilliam Museum, Cambridge.*

Although Oliver's work expressed a sense of English romanticism, his paternal family was originally a long-established dynasty of German Jewish bankers who, in the nineteenth century, were chancellors to the grand duchy of Hesse and financial advisers to both the kaiser in Berlin and the tsar of Russia. Simon Messel, Oliver's great grandfather, studied art in Paris, but on the death of his elder brother, Louis, in 1846, was obliged to head the Messel Bank in Darmstadt. However, his early death from typhoid fever in 1859, at the Solferino battlefield, left his young children fatherless, so the bank was headed by a relative, Ferdinand Sander, and ultimately early in the twentieth century was incorporated into the Deutsche Bank.

Perhaps as a consequence of having to fend for themselves from an early age, Simon's three sons, Ludwig, Rudolph, and Alfred were driven to succeed in their chosen fields. Alfred remained in Germany as an architect, developing his own style of German Classicism. The grand scale of his designs lead him to be known as "The Visionary of the City," and due to his revolutionary use of steel and glass he came to be known as a protomodernist. His best-known buildings were in Berlin, notably the Kaufhaus Wertheim, the largest department store in Europe, and, after his appointment as the kaiser's official architect in 1899, the Pergamon Museum on Berlin's Museum Island with Ludwig Hoffman. He died in 1909. Oliver was aware of his work and in later life was able to visit various projects in Berlin and Darmstadt.

Rudolph, a scientist, settled in England, becoming a Fellow of the Royal Society. His process for the extraction of oleum, a concentrated form of sulphuric acid, was used extensively for industrial purposes such as fabric dyes, explosives, and batteries. To Oliver and his siblings, Rudolph was a genial old man, of whom they were very fond and well worth visiting before the start of each school term as he would slip into their hands a shiny gold sovereign. "Addy" Adamson, Maud's lady's maid, who used to accompany them on visits remarked, "We always went by bus. Mr. Oliver was so polite that I had a job to get him on the bus because he wanted everyone else to get on before him. You used to have to push him on, to get him there, otherwise the bus would be off and he would be standing on the pavement."[1]

Ludwig, who possessed the banking gene, established L. Messel & Co. in 1873, for many years one of London's leading brokerage houses, serving the royal family. His creativity was expressed in the gardens that he and his wife, Anne Cussans, landscaped and planted at their home, Nymans, in Sussex. Oliver regarded him as a "benign but remote Father Christmas figure, with fine features and a head like an El Greco portrait."[2] Their eldest son, Leonard, married Maud Sambourne in 1898, and theirs was a creative marriage, imbued with a sense of connoisseurship and artistic energy.

Maud, a beautiful young girl, was the daughter of Linley Sambourne, the famed illustrator and chief political cartoonist of *Punch* magazine until his death in 1910. She was brought up in their London home, 18 Stafford Terrace, Kensington, now the Linley Sambourne House museum, remarkably unchanged since the 1870s. Here she was

The drawing room on the first floor of 18 Stafford Terrace, Kensington, the Sambournes' London home. Decorated in 1874, it has remained virtually unchanged.

Nymans in Sussex, as remodelled in the years after the First World War by Oliver's parents into their romantic image of a West Country manor house.

OPPOSITE *Maud Messel, Oliver's adored mother, photographed in 1910 at Balcombe House, the early Georgian house which was Oliver's first childhood home and which had a strong influence on him.*

FOLLOWING PAGES
LEFT *Leonard Messel, Oliver's father (described by Oliver as "something of a pocket Napoleon"), as colonel commanding the Fourth Battalion, Royal Sussex Regiment, in 1912.*

RIGHT *Elizabeth Linley by Gainsborough, ca. 1785. Known as the "Nightingale of Bath," she eloped with and married the playwright Richard Sheridan. Mrs. Richard Brinsley Sheridan, ca.1785–87 (oil on canvas) by Thomas Gainsborough (1727–88).*

party to the lively artistic world of her parents and the many leaders in Victorian painting, theatre, and literature that populated it, such as James McNeill Whistler, George Frederick Watts, Henry Irving, Herbert Beerbohm Tree, Henry Rider Haggard, and Oscar Wilde. Linley Sambourne and his wife, Marion, née Herapath, were both keen collectors, cramming their home with an eclectic blend of fashionable antique blue-and-white porcelain and eighteenth-century English furniture.

Collecting was also an enthusiasm embraced by Oliver's parents throughout their lives, and every year their spring travels to Italy, Germany, the Netherlands, and France would be followed months later by the arrival of vans disgorging the carefully wrapped spoils of these tours: furniture, textiles, glass, ceramics, musical instruments, jewellery, porcelain, early continental glass, and especially fans. The fans were collected in a spirit of high seriousness, comprising the finest examples of seventeenth-, eighteenth-, and nineteenth-century European and Asian fans, now part of the Fitzwilliam Museum in Cambridge. The Messels' love for their garden triggered an interest in building a vast collection of herbal manuscripts, some dating from the thirteenth century. These were housed in the library at Nymans but were lost in the great fire that destroyed the house in 1947. The estate was gifted to the National Trust in 1953, and now the gardens surrounding the romantic ruin of the house attract 200,000 visitors a year.

Oliver and his two older siblings were brought up in their parents' rarefied and exotic world, surrounded by beautiful furniture, paintings, and objects in a society cultivated by artists, collectors, connoisseurs, and scholars, both at Lancaster Gate in London and at Balcombe House, his parents' earlier marital home not far from Nymans, in

Sussex. Oliver recalled that he was very happy: "It was a mid eighteenth century Georgian House with front steps that led up to a gallery or Trafalgar balcony, which surrounded three sides of the house. The gallery was covered with jasmine, honeysuckle and roses, giving almost the effect of a welcoming birds nest. That is what first planted in my mind my hankering towards an eighteenth century influence in my work."[3]

Nymans, inherited by Oliver's parents on his grandfather's death in 1915, was viewed by Oliver as "an exceptionally hideous house with a really monstrous conservatory with hardly a redeeming feature except the garden."[4] It was therefore with great reluctance that the family would leave beloved Balcombe House and move to Nymans, but this move was to mark the start of a period of intense creativity for Oliver's mother, who inspired Nymans's transformation into what Christopher Hussey described as "an enchanting house, so clever a reproduction it is of a building begun in the fourteenth century and added to intermittently till Tudor times, that some future antiquary may well be deceived by it."[5]

Whilst at Oxford in the 1890s, Leonard, an artistic and erudite man, established enduring friendships with Max Beerbohm, the caricaturist and wit, and his coterie of fellow dandies and aesthetes. In Oliver's eyes Leonard was "something of a pocket Napoleon, having been spoilt to distraction as a child. To us children, Father's severity, even if only put on for effect, represented something of the King Rat figure. Linley was so scared of him that he never quite got over it, Anne was apprehensive of a brewing tempest. On a few occasions I managed to stand up to him and as fond as we were of each other, it worked, there were great reconciliation scenes."[6]

*Oliver's portrait of his sister,
Anne, and brother-in-law,
Michael, Earl and Countess of
Rosse, at their home, Birr Castle,
Ireland. The ineriors by Anne
Rosse showed much of the style
and exuberance of Oliver's own
interior projects.*

OPPOSITE *Portrait by Horst of
Anne, Countess of Rosse, wearing
a Charles James dress.*

Maud he adored unreservedly as a paragon "of supreme self control and an example to attempt to follow. I never cease to realize fully how amazing this rare inspiration has been, in a faultless being as a mother. Her presence had, as it were, an instant effect upon everyone who came within her orbit." The impression of their mother's Romantic English taste, her ability to beautify, her knowledge of plants and horticulture, her strong creative streak, and her practical abilities in drawing, needlework, and design had a lasting effect on Oliver and Anne.

Maud's father, Linley Sambourne, was born at his mother's home, Bole Hill, at Norton in Derbyshire, the ancestral home of Thomas Linley, and through this the family rejoiced in a connection with the beautiful and musically gifted Linleys of Bath, the most famous of whom were Thomas's son, a composer also called Thomas, the Younger, (a contemporary and friend of Mozart), and his sister Elizabeth, known as "Nightingale of Bath." Her great beauty transfixed Gainsborough, Lawrence, and Reynolds; her unparalleled voice captivated Queen Charlotte and King George III; her chastity infuriated the Prince of Wales; and her charisma so enchanted the playwright Richard Brinsley Sheridan that they eloped and married in 1772. This Linley connection may have lead to the cult of dressing up that infiltrated the Messel home. Leonard and Maud appeared frequently as Richard and Elizabeth Sheridan, whilst their three children never seemed to wear normal clothes. Linley, Anne, and Oliver were frequently transformed into saints, angels, soldiers, knights, kings, jesters, or characters from paintings and history. Oliver's first recollection at the age of four was of "being dressed up as a little French soldier . . . I thought how terribly grown up I was and conscious of feeling it was about time to set out and see the world. I toddled off into the village and hours later somebody found me wandering down by the cricket field. All I wanted to do was explore and be alone. That is the way I felt the rest of my life."[7]

This early sense of independence asserted itself by the time Oliver attended Eton, which followed "the abject misery of being plunged from the pampered life at home to a private school (Hawtreys) of Dickensian horror," where the boys were regularly beaten by the headmaster with birch rods soaked in brine.[8] Strangely Oliver viewed this with a sense of gratitude as he would shut himself off at night from the wretchedness of the daytime world and create for himself a new one. He later wrote, "This may account for my work tending to be imaginative rather than realistic."

Eton he found more acceptable. Here he made lasting friendships with Harold Acton, Brian Howard, Robert Byron, and his cousin, young Rudolph Messel. He regarded Eton very much as a sort of club which he could bob into at his own leisure, as he was able spend much of the term at home, by making himself appear to be a sickly child, a ruse encouraged by his sister, Anne. His letters of this time reveal an aesthetically aware child with a surprisingly sophisticated relationship with his mother. While the letters of most fourteen-year-olds would consist of little more than a humdrum list of school match results, Oliver's letters, addressed to "My own Darling Mother" advised her of books to read, or suggested improvements to make on estate buildings at Nymans, or issued requests for coloured wools (with which he crocheted hats for Anne).

Eton also witnessed Oliver's passion for mimicry and humour, as the author Anthony Powell noted: "John Spencer was standing in a group in the passage when a well-dressed woman walked past. They all took their hats off in the usual way as she moved up the passage and slipped into one of the rooms. Later he went into Oliver Messel's room, and there he was taking tea by himself, dressed as a lady." Oliver possessed enormous personal charm, as well as an ability to make people laugh. Later in life he would be well-known for his parties at which he would perform his hilarious imitations, never unkind, of such characters as his old nanny, with much belching, grunting, and rustling of concealed lavatory paper, or of an English colonel's visit to a Parisian tart.

At the age of seventeen Oliver determined that he was going to be an artist, and that is how he regarded himself all his life. He was enthralled by the paintings of the great Italian Renaissance masters, of Rembrandt, Watteau, Van Dyke, Velázquez, and Veronese, seen on visits to galleries which formed part of his education with his sister. With his mother's friend, the author Gladys Crosier, he would visit the theatrical workshops of her uncle Percy Anderson, where he saw little models and giant canvases on pulleys in an "immense studio, like a composition by Piranesi, rich with the smell of size, with tins and pots of colour dribbling everywhere made a great impression on me."[9]

On other occasions Mr. Lenygon of Lenygon and Morant, specialists in period interior rooms and refurbishers of Buckingham Palace and Windsor Castle who also helped with the decorations at Lancaster Gate and Nymans, would take Oliver "on fascinating expeditions through a maze of Dickensian side streets, to see fabulous materials being woven in Hogarthian surroundings, secret havens for fringes, gimps and tassels, master woodcarvers, gesso work, gilders, glass blowers and engravers."[10] At other times he and Anne would visit their mother's dressmakers, especially Lucy Duff Gordon's Maison Lucile, where they would absorb the techniques for cutting, hanging, and sewing fabrics. This enabled Anne to help Oliver later in cutting and making costumes for his stage designs.

Oliver adored Anne, with whom he shared a particularly close affinity throughout their lives. In many ways they were rather similar, both breathtakingly good-looking, as their photographs by Cecil Beaton attest. Anne, with her patronage of dress designers like Charlie James and Irene Gilbert, shared with Oliver a sense of style and an appreciation of beauty, and both had wills of steel. Anne was regarded as one of the great beauties of her time, an arbiter of fashion, a highly respected gardener, and a wonderful hostess. Her first marriage to the barrister Ronald Armstrong-Jones was short lived, but her marriage to Michael, Earl of Rosse, was one of enduring happiness.

Two friends of Oliver's parents were to have a vital impact on him. One was Archie Propert, a connoisseur in the field of art, author of the first scholarly book on Russian ballet, and part owner of the Claridge Gallery in Brook Street, London. The other was the painter and sculptor Glyn Philpot, who was described by Oliver as having "an imaginative sense of the absurd that would make every moment hilarious and dispel the seriousness or awe of the master. His sense of values was the truest I have ever known, spurning worldly success."[11] They both encouraged Oliver to leave Eton early and to study at the Slade School of Fine Art, in London, under the eminent and austere Professor Henry Tonks. Here he became instant friends with Rex Whistler, with whom he would doodle fantasy baroque palaces and make masks in papier-mâché. Finding the atmosphere of the Slade somewhat like a "railway station," he was apprenticed to John Wells, a portrait painter of distinction, who taught him to study the painting techniques of the Old Masters. Wells, who had a wide circle of friends, introduced him at the Café Royal, then the epicentre of "bohemian" life, to Augustus John, Jacob Epstein, Ambrose McEvoy, and William Orpen.

Masks and their ancient history fascinated Oliver. At weekends he was busy with papier-mâché, pipe cleaners, and gesso, creating a fantasy world of masks. In 1924, at the age of twenty and having left the Slade, he was invited by Archie Propert to exhibit these at his Claridge Gallery.

Oliver's favourite photograph of his beloved companion, Vagn Riis-Hansen, known as the Great Dane, taken by Antony Armstrong-Jones (Earl of Snowdon) at Nymans.

On the opening night he met the great theatrical impresario Sir Charles Cochran, and Serge Diaghilev, director of the Ballets Russes, meetings which would ultimately lead to a career in the theatre. Both men recognized Oliver's talent and arranged for him to work on theatrical productions and revues alongside Georges Braque, Noël Coward, Cole Porter, Ivor Novello, and Max Reinhardt. His success was nearly instantaneous, and soon he was able to establish his own design practice, moving to 16 Yeomans Row, London, which was to be his home and studio for the next twenty-four years.

When Oliver was introduced in 1948 to the handsome Danish couturier and war resistance hero Vagn Riis-Hansen, he modestly described himself as working in stage design. Wishing to promote this young aspirant, Vagn contacted Binky Beaumont, the influential theatrical manager and head of the production company, H. M. Tennent Ltd., who exclaimed, "You bloody fool, Vagn, don't you realize that Oliver Messel is the most famous designer in the world."[12]

This was the start of a devoted friendship, lasting twenty-seven years until Vagn's death. As Oliver's companion, Vagn, affectionately known as "The Great Dane," acted as his manager and organized his life both in their London home, 17 Pelham Place, and later in Barbados, where they moved in 1966. Vagn, with his unique talents for organization and the art of living, was the perfect companion for Oliver. Although Oliver was the highest paid designer, his finances were often in a mess, partly due to his habit of putting payment cheques in a drawer rather than in the bank, a problem which Vagn swiftly resolved. However, money and fragile health (particularly arthritis and angina) would continue to be real anxieties for Oliver throughout his life.

Through Vagn's administrative mastery Oliver was free to concentrate on his work, which followed an idiosyncratic nocturnal schedule, starting after dinner right through the night till dawn the next day. He left endless notes and sketches for his studio team, headed by Mr Potter, located at the top of the house. Vagn was also a great cook who wrote articles on the subject, and organized the most wonderful parties. To make the house run efficiently he organized a staff of five, comprising a Danish cook, butler, and valet, a Barbadian footman, and an English chauffeur.

Oliver looked back on the 1950s as being his most productive and happiest time. As he explained in 1960, "I have liked most of the decades of my life, but the fifties were undoubtedly the best and the most beautiful. It was a wonderfully rich time in the theatre, in fashion, in design.

I think perhaps you get that after a long war — a striving for beauty, a period of excitement and fertility in the arts."[13]

For his work he travelled between London and the U.S., but also he found excitement in visiting more remote places such as Tanzania, Uganda, Albania, and Barbados. He particularly loved Venice, whose rich splendour and lavish parties attracted him each year. In a quiet canal, off Piazza San Marco, he and Vagn would take a house during the summer months. His nephew, the promising young photographer Antony Armstrong-Jones (later Earl of Snowdon), was always a welcome guest. He remembers how he and Oliver would walk all night together observing detail on buildings and watching, before dawn, the city coming to life.

The death of his adored mother in 1960, coupled with his own pain from arthritis and a shift in theatrical taste from romance to "brutalism," prompted Oliver to leave England and move to Maddox, an old plantation house he had bought on the west coast of Barbados. This he transformed with such beauty and imagination that it lead him in a new direction as the architect and creator of many buildings throughout the West Indies, all identified by his own inspired vision of an ideal way for living in the tropics that retains the region's character and charm.

Having started life as a painter, his longing now was to paint, and it was portraiture that he loved most of all, which gave expression to the joy and interest he found in the company of his sitters. Although the theatre held a special place in his heart, painting gave him a sense of freedom from the complications and time pressure of designing enormous theatrical productions. Another of his concerns was the temporary nature of theatre design, which after the show left nothing behind. As he commented to Tony Snowdon, "I have adored doing things for the theatre, but it is a toy — theatre is only a toy, it is an ephemeral thing, whereas painting is not."[14] He did not abandon the idea of stage design but was now very selective about what to take on, his last production being a re-creation in New York of his famous *Sleeping Beauty* for the U.S. bicentenary celebrations in 1976.

My impressions upon arriving from the airport in the evening at Maddox, to be welcomed by Oliver are as fresh today as they were more than thirty-five years ago. The overwhelming sense of joy of seeing him in the setting that he had created was like the effect of great theatre: reaching the house in the evening to find it alive with the gentle glow of candlelight, the Caribbean sea luminescent beyond the dramatically lit "Rousseau-esque" jungle of his garden, and the air full of the scent of frangipani and vibrant

with the chatter of frogs and monkeys. At dinner the green marble tabletop would be festooned with hibiscus and gardenia flowers, and on special occasions Vagn would continue a Danish tradition with a bottle made of frozen petals from which he would pour ice-cold schnapps into little silver cups. After dinner, when all the guests had left, Oliver would retire as always to his studio where he would work until dawn.

On such occasions I would not see Oliver again until before lunch, which was always a light meal, after which he would rest on the chaise longue in the dining room and read to me. Courts and courtesans was a favourite subject of his, racy adventures of the beautiful and seductive Lady Jane Digby amongst German and Greek kings, an Albanian brigand, and Syrian Sheikh Medjuel el Mezrab. Afternoons would be spent visiting craftsmen such as metal workers, stonemasons, cabinet makers, all of whom would be collaborating with him on projects both on Barbados and Mustique. Oliver would show me with pride some of his completed houses or others in progress.

Sometimes in the evenings we would work together in the kitchen. Oliver would cook up a pot of gesso plaster, and I would watch with wonder as he showed me how with a few strings of beads, shells, pipe cleaners, and masking tape he could conjure up a chandelier. We talked ceaselessly, and I treasured everything he said. Oliver was to me more of a friend than an uncle and a creative genius whom I never cease to admire.

Early in the morning of the thirteenth of July 1978, Oliver's charmed life came to an end. Following his meticulous instructions, his and Vagn's ashes were buried together at Nymans, in the walled garden which he had loved so much from childhood. When Oliver went to live in Barbados in 1966, Princess Margaret arranged to store all his work, (over 11,000 items including models, masks, drawings, paintings, and papers) in the old chapel at Kensington Palace, which after his death was cared for by Sir Roy Strong at the Victoria and Albert Museum until acquired in 2005 from Tony Snowdon by the Theatre Museum, which in 2007 became incorporated into the Victoria and Albert Museum. The preservation of this archive gives the unique opportunity for a detailed scrutiny of his work. Over the past few years I have consulted with some of Britain's leading experts in design history, stage design, interior design, architecture, and film design who, like me, have been awestruck by the beauty and scope of Oliver's oeuvre. Our discoveries fill the following pages with proof of Oliver Messel's extraordinary talent and energy.

Oliver with his fawn mask, which caught the eye of Diaghilev and C. B. Cochran, so launching his career in the theatre.

FOLLOWING PAGES
Oliver Messel's oil painting of the walled garden at Nymans, commissioned by his brother, Linley, for the dining room of L. Messel and Company, the brokerage firm founded by their grandfather.

Carolina Herrera

I met Oliver Messel in 1967 and immediately knew that he was all about fantasy, magic, and beauty. Everything he did was a lesson in aesthetics. He was then at the top of his career as a set and costume designer for the ballet, theater, and cinema.

Light-hearted Oliver may have been, but crossed he could become a cobra. I regarded this as a quality that added apprehension to the fun.

The leitmotif in all his productions was style and wit. No detail was ever overlooked, except when he forgot to include a staircase in a lovely palace he was building. He quickly solved the problem by adding a flight of grand outdoor stairs and convinced the owner that she would look so glamorous descending the steps, umbrella in hand, when it rained.

Once when my husband and I arrived at Maddox, I found my room transformed into Sleeping Beauty's enchanted bedroom. In a corner Oliver had re-created an eighteenth-century dressing table, covered in white broderie anglaise and point d'esprit, and the bed, tables, chairs, and windows were all covered and curtained in white.

Carolina Herrera is a fashion designer based in New York.

OPPOSITE *Oliver, the maker of magic.*

Chapter 2

Oliver Messel and Friends

by Stephen Calloway

Our Cartoonist in a Savage Mood — at a Bright Young Party by Anthony Wysard. Drawn in 1930, this is one of Wysard's most elaborate caricatures. Several of Messel's friends are depicted, including Teresa "Baby" Jungman (second from left) and Hugh Lygon (on stairs); Oliver himself (in red, centre) holds two cocktail glasses.

O liver Messel was born into a milieu that was, in the parlance of the day, comfortable, cultured, and connected. His early days were meshed into the seasonal rounds of London Society and country life; however, throughout his career, by a sort of elective affinity, Oliver moved in circles that were to one degree or another artistic, literary, and, in the widest sense, theatrical. Naturally gregarious himself, the people with whom he chose to spend his time were fond of parties and dressing-up, elaborate jokes, gossip, and intrigue. They were, if not always startlingly intellectual and often frighteningly waspish, certainly among the most interesting and almost invariably fun to be with. Within these charmed circles, a good few were titled, a handful were possessed of real originality and talent, whilst, of the rest, most were rich and able to indulge their whims.

Messel and his immediate friends and contemporaries came of age in the 1920s. Theirs was a decade which sought, if not to expunge the memory of the horrors the Great War and of the destruction of the best part of an entire generation of young men, then at least to turn its face from those horrors, seeking consciously to create a new world by devoting the greatest energy to frivolity. Crucially, too, the terrible slaughter of the war left the boys, such as

ABOVE *Oliver Messel and Gerald Berners, composer, writer, painter, and joker, photographed at a fairground booth, probably in Italy, about 1930.*

OPPOSITE *Oliver Messel with his masks for Noël Coward's "Dance Little Lady" in C. B. Cochran's revue* This Year of Grace, *1928.*

Oliver, Rex Whistler, and Cecil Beaton, all born between 1904 and 1905, to grow up both largely free in their ambitions from the usual oppressive rivalry of an immediately previous generation and indulged to an unusual degree by their elders. Probably no era since that of the ancien régime in France so strenuously embraced a life devoted to pleasure. Frenetically social, the most serious aim of these young men — and the women — of Messel's generation, the "Bright Young People" as they came to be known, seemed to be a headlong pursuit of amusement.

At each stage of his career, during school days at Eton, at the Slade School of Fine Art, and later, as the 1920s gave way to the 1930s and Messel began to make his way in the theatre, he seemed to have a talent for being at the centre of things. In the heady, fashionable world of London between the wars, he was constantly in demand whether designing stage sets, masks, and costumes or contriving equally lavish effects for parties for his smart friends. By the late 1940s and into the 1950s, as others from his background struggled to adapt to a very changed postwar scene, Messel's continuing inventiveness kept his name at the fore. Later still, in the 1960s, as taste moved again to embrace fantasy and peacock elegance, his sense of style and irrepressible charm won him new admirers of a much younger generation. Like his great friend and competitor Cecil Beaton, now remembered best as the photographer and diarist who chronicled the age of elegance, Oliver had a mercurial ability to reinvent himself. By the 1970s, although Oliver now lived the whole time in Barbados, and Cecil, following a stroke, seldom left Reddish, his Wiltshire house, they remained friends; both had become objects of curiosity as survivors from the Jazz Age.

It was during that golden age, almost exactly half a century earlier, when Messel and Beaton had first met. For much of that eventful period of time their careers, their social connections, and even their love-lives had either run in closest parallel or at times become curiously intertwined. It is significant that their most important patrons and supporters, their close friends and also their enemies were by and large drawn from the same social circles. Many of their dramas, their highs and lows, their many triumphs, and their occasional ludicrous moments were played out amid the same cast of characters, against the same backdrops, and in that novel glare of publicity which they consciously attracted and in which they both revelled.

Like many sensitive, highly strung, somewhat feminine boys raised in households in which mothers and sisters played a significant part, both Oliver and Cecil found their

first experiences of school a harsh shock. For Messel, escape from the tortures of his "hellish" prep school made arrival at Eton seem relatively congenial. Joining his cousin Rudolph Messel, he entered Mr. Robeson's, "an old, tough house," which according to the novelist Anthony Powell "accommodated ['Billy'] Clonmore [later Earl of Wicklow] . . . and several others with claims to unconventionality and raffishness."[1] Quick-witted, good-looking, and with a talent for drawing and satirical impersonations of masters and other boys, Oliver quickly established himself as a popular and amusing figure. At this time, Messel, Clonmore — described as possessing a "fearful skill at dealing with enemies" — and a third friend, Robert Byron, became firm allies in rebellion.[2]

Along with contemporaries including Alan Clutton-Brock, the future art historian; John Sutro, another accomplished mimic; and Ian Fleming, the creator of James Bond, they gravitated naturally toward the brilliant artistic set that gathered around the Acton brothers, William and Harold, and Brian Howard, "the most fashionable boy in the school."[3] These aesthetes were to become a notable force, both during their days at Eton and later when several of their number would regroup at Oxford. Cyril Connolly, at first something of an outsider, described them admiringly as "a set of boys who were literary and artistic but too lazy to gargle quotations and become inoculated with the virus of good taste latent in Eton teaching." Brian Howard, a flamboyant dandy, flaunted a very carefully cultivated archness later memorably characterised by Evelyn Waugh as a "ferocity of elegance." In his typical style, obviously influenced by the flippant pose of the dandy-novelist Ronald Firbank, Howard wrote, "Haven't done any extra work as I have been *plagued* with people. Oliver Messel comes to my room and eats up all my cake. Order white spats. Really too hot for any additional study. Order lovely tie, new patent leather shoes, lovely new suit." Harold Acton in his *Memoirs of an Aesthete* recalled that the aesthetes' enemies, the athletes and "hearties," "resented our gaiety and feared our repartee."

When Messel declared his firm intention of becoming an artist, the example of his grandfather Linley Sambourne, a cartoonist for *Punch*, though hardly himself a wild bohemian, must have been reassuring to the family. Oliver was given every encouragement to pursue his chosen course and, whilst it would never become the main focus of his activity, he did in fact become a good painter, excelling at carefully observed figure and portrait studies. In this genre he was greatly influenced later by the friendship and guid-

Daphne du Maurier sitting for her portrait by Oliver Messel, early 1930s.

ance of Glyn Philpot, a highly regarded society portraitist who later espoused the modernist cause. Philpot also shared Oliver's predilection for the beauty of black models, but initially, having enrolled at the Slade, then widely regarded as the best of the art schools, Messel found himself subjected to the rigorous regime of drawing, first from antique casts and then the life model, as prescribed by Professor Henry Tonks, the benign dictator who had nurtured the talents of generations of fine draughtsmen, including Augustus John and Henry Lamb and marshalled the increasing band of women artists who, excluded from most other art schools of the day, became known as the "Sladey Ladies."

At the Slade, Oliver immediately became friendly with another student, Rex Whistler, a quiet but captivatingly charming genius with an endless flow of artistic inventiveness that in Tonk's judgment easily outweighed his seeming inability to draw with any success the plaster casts or models actually before his eyes. In a letter to his new friend, Whistler wrote "the Antique [Room] presents a most terrifying spectacle to anyone with the courage to open the door . . . one packed vista of orderly and artistic ladies in serried rank upon rank — peppered sparsely with the more sombre hues of diligent and intimidated males. A veritable phalanx of industrious scholars . . ."

Cecil Beaton posing before the Renaissance portal of Old Wardour Castle, during an expedition from nearby Ashcombe.

OPPOSITE *Marlene Dietrich photographed in Hollywood. Oliver thought her "ravishing" in* Shanghai Express.

Two weeks late and characteristically unwilling to cut short a holiday until after the term had begun, a third new arrival joined them: Stephen Tennant, gilded scion of one of the great families of late nineteenth-century intellectual aristocrats, whose mother, Pamela, was remarried to the political grandee Lord Grey of Fallodon. Messel, Whistler, and Tennant found each other's company congenial and when not in classes ate their lunchtime sandwiches together under the portico of the college or lounged in the quad reading aloud from their favourite Romantic poets. Rex's brother Laurence Whistler recalled Stephen's etiolated appearance at that time as "like a more delicate Shelley." Together they explored London, discovering "Hogarthian alleyways," delighting in forgotten corners such as Wapping Old Stairs, and seeking out architectural gems like the York Water Gate, then still ruinously neglected.[4] Though very distinct characters with such differences in their backgrounds and social circles, ambitions and skills, they became remarkably close. Stephen in particular and of course Oliver both had extremely privileged upbringings, whilst Rex came from more modest origins; on the other hand, it could be said that Rex and Oliver were both possessed of striking artistic talent, but that Stephen as an overindulged child had ideas far beyond his ability and a fatal inherent languor. By contrast again, Rex had a powerful determination to succeed, which was nearly matched — to the surprise of many of his friends — by Oliver's.

It was at Stephen's family house Wilsford that many of the Bright Young People gathered. At weekend parties they played games, made amateur films, and, crucially, began to form a series of interrelated friendships that would ultimately link many of the key writers, artists, and designers of the period. Regular visitors included not only Rex and Oliver but also Cecil Beaton, the wildly social Jungman sisters Teresa (called "Baby") and Zita, and amusing figures of a slightly older generation, including Siegfried Sassoon (Stephen's lover for a while), Edith Olivier, the Sitwell brothers Osbert and Sacheverell, and their protégé William Walton. On one memorable occasion Osbert Sitwell took a party from Wilsford over to nearby Ham Spray House to visit Lytton Strachey, several of them still wearing the fancy costumes they had donned for filmmaking. Always susceptible to the charms of the well-bred young, Strachey was enchanted to meet these "strange creatures — with just a few feathers where brains should be."[5]

The group that coalesced at this time would, however, prove far from inconsequential. It is no exaggeration to say that the friendship that grew up between Messel, Beaton, Whistler, and Tennant was of the greatest significance.

Oliver Messel and his sister, Anne, in fancy dress for a party; Oliver wears the celebrated white and silver classical costume he designed for Paris in Helen!

Oliver Messel in New York with Diana Vreeland, the formidable editor of Vogue.

BELOW *Bianca Macias photographed by Oliver during a visit with Mick Jagger.*

Oliver's sister, Anne, in the garden at Nymans with Edward James, poet and millionaire collector of the Surrealists.

ABOVE *Penelope Tree, girlfriend of the photographer David Bailey and one of the most enigmatic faces of the 1960s, photographed by Oliver at Maddox.*

LEFT *Barbara "Babe" Paley, wife of William S. Paley and one of the luminaries of New York society.*

43

Indeed, the complex ramifications of this central friendship and the intricate pattern of shifting relationships that grew up around it between their various friends and acquaintances was to be of real importance to the world of art and the theatre and came to affect the very warp and weft of London society in the 1920s and 1930s.

Oliver's connection with the aesthetes of his Eton school days —"a galaxy of individual and eccentric personalities," as he called them — was renewed when he was summoned to join them for increasingly sophisticated weekend junketings in Oxford, many of them staged in the infamously bohemian Hypocrites Club. This hard-drinking undergraduate society (named from the manifest hypocrisy of the club motto: "water's best") was housed rather distantly from smarter and more respectable Oxford institutions in ramshackle premises above a bicycle shop in St. Aldates. Messel's friends Hugh Lygon, Robert Byron, the Actons, and Brian Howard, now joined by Evelyn Waugh and other dissolute characters, had somehow managed to take over the Hypocrites from the incumbent hearty set and introduced a decidedly decadent flavour that increasingly aroused the suspicions of the university authorities. Even the club servant observed wryly "they call themselves artists; all they draw is corks."

In London, with his career as a designer for the theatre taking off largely due to the enthusiastic patronage of the impresario C. B. Cochran, Oliver became swept up in a whirl of activity in which work and parties seemed to feed off each other. His friends were also meeting with success: Whistler had painted his Tate Gallery restaurant murals to great acclaim and was much in demand (Tonks declared "there will be a boom in Whistler"), and Beaton was meanwhile rapidly gaining recognition for his highly original photographic portraits. In April 1928, for his twenty-second birthday, Stephen Tennant threw a party in conjunction with Brenda Dean Paul, "the society drug addict." Her cousin Olivia Wyndham, Oliver, Cecil, and Rex all attended, as did the Oxford aesthetes and a new influx of chic theatre people such as the camp actor Ernest Thesiger. As host, Stephen wore "diamond earrings and a football jersey," a look that was gleefully reported by Tom Driberg writing as "William Hickey," the society columnist for the *Daily Express.* From this moment the glare of publicity was on the Bright Young People and their ever more bizarre novelty parties. Their amusements and indiscretions increasingly became public property, and it has been plausibly suggested (by Martin Green and others) that a number of "insiders" such as Driberg and, of course,

Evelyn Waugh (in his novel *Vile Bodies*) but also Beverley Nichols, Noël Coward, Cecil Beaton, and Messel all began in their various ways to enjoy some considerable degree of wider social success and financial reward by selling the aristocratic-dandy-aesthete ideal to an essentially bourgeois and philistine but highly receptive public.

Moving with increasing assurance in a widening circle of friends, celebrities, and notorious characters, Messel, Beaton, and Whistler often found themselves in rivalry both in terms of work and their social lives. Both Rex and Oliver accepted invitations to travel to Italy with the eccentric genius Lord Berners (Gerald Tyrwhitt), "the versatile peer." Writer, artist, musician, collaborator with Diaghilev, and the inspiration for Lord Merlin in Nancy Mitford's books, Berners owned a delightful, small baroque house in Rome, which on arrival his young guests discovered had only a single bedroom. A more extended emotional tangle was played out in the full glare of public scrutiny when both Oliver and Cecil fell in love with the rich but melancholic Peter Watson, a young Maecenas who collected paintings by Picasso and later owned and funded both *Horizon* magazine and *Poetry London*. Meeting Watson by chance en route to Venice, Cecil developed a lasting though probably entirely unrequited passion. Oliver, who liked to describe himself as a mischief-maker and perhaps largely in order to amuse his own vanity and best Cecil, took a doubly cruel delight in playing with Watson's affections. Oliver and Cecil in one terrible scene on the day of Diana Cooper's birthday at the Lido, "fought like bears." Berners captured something of the flavour of this hothouse world of homosexual rivalry and intense friendships in *The Girls of Radcliffe Hall,* his *roman à clef* cast in the form of a hilariously malicious spoof on girls' school stories.

In what must still have been a potential explosive scene, in 1930 Oliver, Peter Watson, and Rex Whistler were the first guests to stay at Ashcombe, the Wiltshire house which Beaton leased and transformed into a magical retreat for weekend amusements. Here, as at nearby Wilsford, friends and an increasingly starry cast of acquaintances from theatre and film and the literary and artistic world gathered for lazy reading afternoons, impromptu expeditions, and picnics, all recorded by Cecil's camera or on amateur movie film. Exotic Tilly Losch, the dancer whom Oliver had dressed as the sublime Manchu Marchioness in Cochran's *Wake Up and Dream,* and her husband, Edward James, the millionaire art-collector, brought Salvador Dalí. On other occasions the socialite interior decorators Syrie Maugham or Sybil Colefax came, on others Greta Garbo, with whom Cecil fell in love,

The actress and singer Jacqui Chan and Tom Parr, interior decorator and business partner of David Hicks.

or Tallulah Bankhead, with whom Rex Whistler had an affair (a prize no less to be valued though so widely awarded by her, as his brother rather sourly remarked). The great culmination of the Ashcombe years was Beaton's celebrated three-day fancy-dress *fête champêtre*, an event so stylish, so extravagant, and so memorable that in some ways it formed the high-water mark of an entire era.

The decorations and furnishings at Ashcombe were in a light and whimsical style that blended those same elements of Baroque and Rococo, tinged with Victoriana and refracted through the lens of Surrealism, that characterised Cecil's photographs, Rex's paintings, and Oliver's stage sets and costumes at this moment. The most concerted scheme was that of Cecil's "Circus" bedroom in which the chairs were shaped like drums with drumstick arms and — surely as a knowing joke — his elaborately carved four-

poster bed was cast in the form of a merry-go-round. The walls of the room were adorned all around with a sequence of trompe l'oeil niches containing images of circus folk. These were painted by Oliver, Gerald Berners, and Beaton himself, and by Rex, who created the best, a superb circus strong woman. Photographs of the painters at work also record the presence of another friend of their circle, a German artist named Raimund von Hofmannsthal but it is recorded that his contribution did not find favour and was discreetly painted out and replaced by Whistler, the only thoroughly competent muralist of the group.

By this date both Oliver and Cecil had many American friends and, like a good few young English writers, artists, and designers, found their talents courted in New York and Hollywood. Both were excited not just by the possibilities of working in the theatre and in films, but also by the new

social contacts that such employment brought. In addition to mixing with stars such as Marlene Dietrich and Katherine Hepburn, Messel also found himself drawn into wealthy social circles in which he began regularly to encounter such figures such as the heiress Doris Duke and the beautiful Paleys. Oliver in particular enjoyed expeditions to Harlem, where the American writer and photographer Carl Van Vechten acted as his guide into the exciting world of black singers and entertainers that had first intrigued him back in 1927, when the celebrated Florence Mills brought *The Blackbirds* revue to London. *The Blackbirds* had opened in New York and subsequently had been popular in Paris, but in London it ran triumphantly for a year, during which time Oliver had thrown a party at which, as one gossip column noted, "all the Oxford Brian Howard set" had befriended several members of the troupe.[6]

For Messel, as for Beaton and Whistler, the 1930s were years of great success, not least because their style, essentially lighthearted, romantic, and escapist, fitted so precisely the mood of the times. However, as the decade progressed and the international situation became more ominous, a sense of foreboding became noticeable. With the rise of Hitler — of whom Oliver had oddly once taken an informal snapshot whilst on holiday in Bavaria — political realists began to talk of the inevitability of a European war, and even the most determined hedonists and head-in-the-sand optimists were obliged to recognise that an era was coming to an end. One of the last great extravagances before the storm was the Jersey Ball, a huge eighteenth-century-themed costume party held at Osterley Park at the end of the social season, in the summer of 1939. Lady Jersey, an American and, before her marriage, a star of the

ABOVE LEFT *Socialite Elsa Maxwell and Maria Callas.*

ABOVE RIGHT *Lady Diana Cooper in the Cleopatra costume based on Tiepolo's fresco, designed for her by Oliver and Cecil Beaton to wear at Charles de Beistegui's ball at Palazzo Labia in Venice, September 1951.*

LEFT *The Hon. Daisy Fellowes
and her attendant, dressed for
the Beistegui Ball, posing
before the great Tiepolo fresco
at Palazzo Labia.*

RIGHT *Guests, including Syrie
Maugham (left), costumed for
the Jersey Ball at Osterley Park
House, the last great social event
of the season in the summer of
1939.*

*Oliver Messel in his Yeoman's
Row studio, surrounded by masks
made for Cochran revues and
other theatrical productions.*

early cinema, wore a dress of silver and blue silk brocade designed by Oliver. One thousand revellers enjoyed
the lavish settings created by Messel with the help of the
brilliant decorator and pasticheur Felix Harbord and were
entertained by sideshows devised by the ever-inventive
film producer John Sutro. Oliver himself appeared in an
immaculate embroidered suit and carefully coiffed wig,
only to be outdone by Cecil in a vast Ramillies peruke and
eighteenth-century high heels.

The declaration of war did not at first bring social and
cultural life to a complete stop. Though lavish entertain-
ments ceased, the theatre and ballet continued, and both
Oliver and Rex contrived, after joinig forces, to design stage
productions, and they and Cecil all managed to carry out
other artistic commissions during the strange uncertain
period of the Phoney War. Oliver was commissioned into the
Camouflage Corps as a captain; Cecil, working on aircraft
recognition duties, was pictured in *Tatler* magazine in an
immaculately tailored uniform, toying with photographs of
warplanes laid out on his drawing-room floor. Rex, unlike
the other two and many of the rest of their circle who found
desk jobs or work with Intelligence, determined to serve in
a regular unit. Refusing the entreaties of his friends to do
something safer such as becoming a war artist, he was eventually commissioned as a junior officer in the Welsh Guards
to train as a troop leader in the armoured brigade. He was
tragically killed on his first day in action in June 1944 during the major tank advance shortly after the D-Day landings.

The loss of one of the most brilliant and beloved of their
friends was keenly felt by all in the circle and only slowly
did life begin to get back to normal. At his Yeomans Row
house and later with his move to Pelham Place in South
Kensington close to Cecil Beaton and Felix Harbord, the
gaiety of existence gradually began to reassert itself for
Oliver. In addition to survivors from the prewar days,
Oliver also began to gather about him new and congenial
friends such as the theatrical photographer Angus McBean
(known as "One-shot McBean" for his speed and precision
at photo shoots) and Martin Battersby, a talented painter
who served at various times as an assistant (and occasion-
ally more, perhaps) for all the Pelham gang. Tony
Armstrong-Jones, Oliver's nephew and a budding photographer — though working in a grittier and more realistic
and modern manner than the Messel-Beaton neo-Roman-
tic vein — also became an important figure at this time.

A great signal of the return of glamour came in 1951
when the Chilean millionaire Charles de Beistegui
announced that he intended to celebrate the restoration of

the Palazzo Labia in Venice with a lavish ball. Beistegui
had lived in Paris since the 1920s when he had commissioned an ultramodern apartment from Le Corbusier. But
rapidly tiring of the austere aesthetic, he had devoted his
considerable energies and vast fortune to buying houses
and amassing staggeringly opulent collections of Baroque
objects. Taking the celebrated Tiepolo frescoes of the Labia
palace as the theme for the ball, all was conceived on an
epic scale. The whole of smart European pre- and postwar
society gathered to watch Diana Cooper, attired as Cleopatra in a superb and daring Messel gown, arrive by gondola.
"Don Carlos" de Beistegui, casting himself in the role of an
eighteenth-century doge, managed no fewer than three costume changes throughout the evening, whilst as usual
Oliver and Cecil vied for attention, with the laurels this
time going to Oliver for his coat of crimson velvet once
worn by a Bavarian princeling.

The Beistegui ball represented for some a welcome return
to the opulence and lavish style of the interwar years, but
for many it was seen as the last gasp of an era that very soon
would cease to exist. The smart world of the 1950s and
1960s would be very different: less aristocratic, certainly,
and whilst still influenced by wealth, increasingly animated
by the new kind of celebrity that came with careers in films
and now television. Perhaps because he bridged those
worlds, Oliver found little difficulty in making the transition
from an old world of grandees and duchesses to that of media
darlings such as Maria Callas, the first great opera diva of
the new era. Along with old friends such as Noël Coward
and the mysterious Alexis, Baron de Redé, Oliver joined the
new "jet set" with the same alacrity with which decades earlier he had once embraced the Bright Young People.

As has been suggested, Messel shared with Cecil
Beaton an extraordinary talent to reinvent himself. Like
Beaton, in the 1960s he found himself an object of fasci-
nation to a generation who were intrigued by the *Wun-
derkind* tradition. Christopher Gibbs, the antique dealer,
éminence grise of the peacock dandies, and connoisseur of
rare souls, introduced Mick Jagger, David Bailey, and their
circle to the recherché glamour of the world of Oliver and
Cecil. Toward the end, in one of Beaton's last diary entries
to mention him, made on 12 January 1974, he wrote "The
birthday (70th) of Oliver Messel my great rival of so long
standing. He has made a wonderful new life for himself in
the West Indies and in spite of great illness shows himself
to be a mighty strong character and personality." To this
almost obituary-like observation Beaton appended a most
uncharacteristic final note: "I am fond of him."[7]

Sir Roy Strong

Oliver Messel and Cecil Beaton were the twin stars in my firmament when, just after the war, I awoke to the magic of theatre. Both had risen to prominence, along with Rex Whistler, in the 1930s, but Whistler had been killed in 1944. The two that remained were to enjoy a heyday of just about a decade and a half, when they too went into eclipse. Both were dramatically affected by the revolution in the drama epitomised by Look Back in Anger (1956) and that in stage design by the mechanistics of Sean Kenny.

Messel's productions vanished from the stage; his memory was gradually eroded. A revival of interest in him began with the exhibition I staged at the Victoria and Albert Museum in 1983 on the occasion of the museum accepting his complete archive, which had been stored at Kensington Palace.

Messel's work will always remain impossible to reevoke as perception has moved on and there is so little of his that can now be seen beyond his wispy designs and papery stage models. It is hoped that this publication will reassert someone who, in his time, was neither wispy nor papery but a major presence in the history of British theatre design.

Sir Roy Strong is an English art historian, museum curator, writer, broadcaster, and landscape designer.

OPPOSITE Oliver Messel and Cecil Beaton reunited in the garden of Messel's house in Pelham Place.

Chapter 3

Messel on Stage

by Sarah Woodcock

*Messel's bewitching evocation
of the Orient seen through
eighteenth-century European
eyes can be seen in the garden
of Bassa Selim's palace in* Die
Entführung aus dem Serail,
Glyndebourne, 1956, with Kevin
Miller as Pedrillo
and Arnold van Mill as Osmin.
The tortoise is a characteristically
charming and witty Messel touch.

O liver Messel's theatre designs oozed glamour, and not the superficial glamour of Hollywood, but the alluring poetic glamour of bewitchment and enchantment, transforming the familiar into something rich and strange. He was seemingly a mass of contradictions — a romantic but with a cool logic and practical common sense; Britain's first star designer, capable of stealing the notices from author, director, and actors, yet who worked best as part of a creative team; a painter at heart, whose paintings became stage pictures which mirrored the creative ideas of the author. In other words, he had the ideal qualities to make a great stage designer.

When Messel was born, the stage designer, in the modern sense, didn't exist. Realism still ruled the stage: sets were devised by skilled craftsmen; scene painters and costumes were either based on historic dress, or supplied by a fashionable dressmaker. Then, in 1909, the success of Sergei Diaghilev's Ballets Russes consolidated a growing trend to use painters as designers, and gradually literal realism was replaced by designs in which mood and emotion were conveyed by an imaginative distillation of reality.

With no formal training, many of the new generation of stage designers trained as painters, Messel among them, but he became stage designer first and painter second. He learned on the job, but saw this as an advantage: "I think, in a way, that the less you know technically, the more you know. Your mind must imagine first, then get over the technical difficulties."[1]

A costume design for Fatima in Zémire et Azor, 1955.

Lubov Tchernicheva as a Muse in Zéphyr et Flore, *1925, with the Messel-designed mask. He also created some "grotesques propped about the décor."*

Certainly he never lacked confidence. He actually turned down his first commission from C. B. Cochran, because it meant realising someone else's designs, so his theatrical debut was for Diaghilev, creating masks for Léonide Massine's 1925 ballet *Zéphyr et Flore*, designed by Braque. "Even at that time," he admitted, "I was a bit of a prima donna."

Learning on the job had definite advantages when that meant working for Cochran, who nurtured a generation of writers, composers, and designers. Over the next five years, Messel created occasional scenes in Cochran's stylish, topical, witty revues, absorbing every aspect of a theatrical production, experimenting with materials and effects, learning to grasp the essentials of a script and embody it in succinct visual terms and to work as part of a team. But a highly individual "Messel" was there from the start.

His debut designs for "The Masks" in *Cochran's 1926 Revue* showed his feeling for heightened realism. His masks for "Dance Little Lady" in *This Year of Grace*, perfectly meshed with Noël Coward's caustic summation of the Bright Young Things. For Cochran they "faithfully reproduced the mirthless, vacuous expressions that could be seen any night in smart restaurants and clubs, where empty-looking youths danced with empty-looking girls in an empty shuffle."[2] James Laver called it a "modern dance of death."[3]

"Manchu Marchioness" in *Wake Up and Dream* achieved maximum effect with minimal means: a red Chinese bridge against a shimmering bluish-green background, by which stood a figure seemingly made of glazed porcelain, an effect achieved by painting a fine layer of rubber onto a specially woven fabric so that it fell heavily in inflexible folds. While using new materials, Messel was also wildly inventive: "Every time I saw him," Cochran recalled, "he would pull something new out of his pocket — usually something used for domestic work — which he proposed to employ to give the illusion of some other fabric."[4] When he first experimented with white (a taboo colour in theatre) in "Heaven" in *Cochran's 1930 Revue*, he broke down the stark white of the costumes with charlady's swabs, loofahs, and bath scrubbers, using an apricot-tinted makeup to counteract the draining effect of white on the face. He was always a master of surface texture.

In 1932 Cochran entrusted Messel with a complete production. *Helen!* was A. P. Herbert's ingenious updating of *La Belle Hélène*, Offenbach's satire on French Second Empire morals based on the Helen of Troy myth. Messel gathered a formidable team, including director Max Reinhardt, choreographer Massine, and stars George Robey and

OPPOSITE *Design for Lady Sneerwell in* The School for Scandal, *Copenhagen, 1958. Messel softened the boldness of the green and orange with characteristic eighteenth-century frills and feathers.*

Design for Oberon in A Midsummer Night's Dream, *Old Vic, 1937. The costume was likened to a shimmering stag-beetle, gleaming and glistening under stage lights.*

Evelyn Laye. As Herbert remarked, there was a danger that "the pot would boil over from sheer excess of personality."[5] Although the least known, Messel almost stole the show with a virtuoso performance which remained true to Offenbach while skilfully fusing Greek temples, Baroque colonnades, Rococo drapes, Empire bedrooms, and Louis XIV carousels while poking fun at classical and nineteenth-century costumes with witty references to his own times. Every night the audience gasped as the curtain rose on Helen's dazzling white bedroom with its swan-guarded bed. Almost overnight fashionable London interiors were transformed from oriental and brilliant colours (the legacy of Léon Bakst's designs for the Ballets Russes), to white, white, and white. And not just in London: "I am off to India to paint the Black Hole of Calcutta *white*," declared Syrie Maugham, and in Hollywood, a friend told Messel, "she's white-washing the whole of the film colony."[6]

The brittle sophistication of the 1920s died with the Depression, and the theatre reflected the growing nostalgia for the security and confidence of pre-1914 England. Messel proved himself as adept at nostalgia as smart chic, creating 750 costumes for the pageant play *The Miracle*, originally produced in 1912. Ivor Novello's *Glamorous Night* was an unashamed marriage between Viennese operetta and realistic nineteenth-century staging. *A Midsummer Night's Dream* was pastiche Victorian, with Mendelssohn's incidental music and fairies in gauzy ballet dresses but typically Messel in the fantastical lush foliage that dwarfed the actors. Particularly noteworthy were iridescent, beetle-like Oberon and Titania's crown, its coloured foil flowers and opalescent cellophane "uprights" magical in effect and entirely practical in its weightlessness.

In 1946 he achieved the extraordinary feat of transforming *The Sleeping Beauty*, greatest of Russian classical ballets, into a mistily romantic vision of Englishness that shone like a beacon of hope in an era of drab austerity. Responding to the audience's need for visual stimulation, he created memorable designs for *The Lady's Not for Burning*, Christopher Fry's poetic drama hailed as a new way forward for British theatre, and forged a fruitful collaboration with the brilliant young director Peter Brook, notably in *Ring Round the Moon*, Fry's adaptation of Jean Anouilh's *L'Invitation au château*.

It was Pygmalion meets Cinderella but with twin contrasting princes, and the Brook-Messel conception of Anouilh's delicate "charade with music" was well-nigh perfect. Messel's miniature Crystal Palace soared gossamer-

like against a springtime evening sky, "floating it seemed on the fantastic airs of the comedy itself."[7] He reunited with Brook for the musical *House of Flowers*, his sets radiating a languid dreaminess which mitigated the more unpleasant aspects of a story of the rivalry between two brothels, with voodoo ceremonies, carnival, a seemingly fatal abduction, and drunken revels. In Messel's sun-beaten tropical idyll "enormous sunflower vines smirk from the facade of Madame Fleur's,"[8] lushly decadent flora crawled lovingly over the sun-blistered, faded facades, and a morning glory gramophone horn loomed over the drawing room.

During the 1950s, Messel consolidated his reputation as an opera designer, particularly at Glyndebourne, making a stand for imaginative realism before the dead hand of neorealism and the frantic quest to update opera became fashionable. In a play the initial impact is made by the designer as the curtain rises, but in opera and ballet the mood is set by the overture; following Mozart, Rossini, and Richard Strauss can be daunting, but Messel met them on their own terms. His great achievement was when four of his productions were performed during the Mozart bicentennial in 1956 — *Idomeneo*, *Il Nozze di Figaro*, *Die Zauberflöte*, and *Die Entführung aus dem Serail* — each a unique world perfectly in accord with Mozart's vision. *Idomeneo*, a static opera seria, had long been thought unstageable, but Messel's vision of mythical Crete transmuted through the eyes of Tiepolo helped turn it into a triumph and secured its place in the operatic repertory. For *Die Entführung aus dem Serail*, he studied not only original Moorish miniatures, carpets, and buildings but how they had been interpreted in European decorative arts, like Meissen porcelain or the Residenz at Munich; the result was a joyous, witty confection which "chime[s] inevitably with the tsing-ching-book of Mozart's so-called Turkish choruses."[9]

He succeeded equally with Rossini. In the palace ante-room of *La Cenerentola*, the visual tempo of the flowing arches perfectly complemented the flow of Rossini's brilliant rhythms and comic invention, while for *Le Comte Ory* he created a toy-theatre set which wittily contained both the fluid languidness of the women, reminiscent of figures on a Gobelin tapestry, and the knockabout humour of the men.

Unsurprisingly, he was out of sympathy with the new drama of the 1950s, which, ironically, demanded a realism akin to that rejected by Messel's generation. His one foray into the new world was Lionel Bart's 1965 musical

Set model showing the exterior of the Harem in Die Entführung aus dem Serail, *Glyndebourne, 1956. Messel reflected the exuberant virtuosity of Mozart's music in fantastic foliage and a structure which might have been piped from icing sugar. The arching golden palm tree appeared in every set, interior as well as exterior.*

Set model for Act I of Il Barbiere
di Siviglia, *Glyndebourne, 1959.
Messel's conscious artificiality
perfectly matches Rossini's light
touch in his parody of social
behaviour.*

Set model for Act II of Il Barbiere
di Siviglia, *Glyndebourne, 1954.
Messel often created visual
tension by setting rooms at an
angle to the proscenium arch.*

Set model for a hall in Faninal's House, in Der Rosenkavalier, *Glyndebourne, 1954, which perfectly translates the Rococo style into stage terms. The chandelier is suggested by shaped acetate, painted white and sequined.*

Set model for Idomeneo, *Glyndebourne, 1951. The colonnades, built in partial relief, and the steep perspectives are reminiscent of Palladio's Teatro Olimpico in Vicenza.*

69

Twang!!, directed by the innovative left-wing Joan Littlewood, but the project was unsympathetic to both Messel and Littlewood, and there was no way they could establish a rapport. After its failure, Messel abandoned the stage, returning only in 1974 to design costumes for the stage version of Lerner and Lowe's *Gigi*, which rivalled Cecil Beaton's Oscar-winning film designs in inventiveness, wit, and charm.

Messel's love of the eighteenth century and the acclaim and longevity of *The Sleeping Beauty* have tended to obscure his remarkable range. Few designers have equally mastered drama, opera, ballet, musicals, and revue. Although a Messel style was unmistakable, there were as many different Messels as productions he designed: medieval in *The Lady's Not for Burning*, Renaissance for *Romeo and Juliet*, Restoration in *The Country Wife*, Russian in *Queen of Spades*, Caribbean in *House of Flowers*. The operatic fantasy of

Zémire et Azor differed from the romantic fantasy of *Ring Round the Moon* just as the satirical fantasy of *Under the Sycamore Tree* differed from the sophisticated fantasy of *The Little Hut*. He matched visually the elegance of Sheridan and the chic of Cochran's revues, and deftly encompassed Cocteau, Fry, Anouilh, Shakespeare, Wycherley, Rossini, Richard Strauss, and Mozart.

Nymans, Messel's family home, was an important influence. The house was an ingenious welding of old and new into a personal vision of the Jacobean; the garden is of national importance yet retains "an intimate charm. It is this unusual combination of the rare and the exotic with the simple and the friendly that is so unusual and so remarkable."[10] Messel's stage designs, too, were of the present but consciously looking back, grand yet accessible with the cunningly contrived naturalism of a Repton or Capability Brown. Like them, he created distant vistas, landscape or townscape, leading the eye outward, suggesting a world beyond the immediate stage action.

A Messel-designed production was not just distinguished by beauty, imaginative strength, wit, elegance, inventiveness, and taste, but exuded a sense of *rightness* so powerful as to seem inevitable. The designs fitted into the production like a cog in a superb machine, dovetailing into the whole, beautiful because fit for the purpose. As the curtain rose, his sets enveloped performer and audience, drawing them into the world of the play. *The Little Hut*'s ebulliently witty, exotic vegetation prepared the audience for a sophisticated comedy, while his Tony-award-winning forest in *Rashomon* was as ineffably mysterious as the action and as much a protagonist as any of the characters. The room as refuge in *The Lady's Not for Burning* was implied by allowing glimpses of the outside world that has shaped the action and characters through the high, Gothic

windows — though for once Messel's practicality failed him and the set's realistic perspective didn't provide a proper exit through the centre door, condemning four actors to spend twenty minutes cramped in a cubbyhole until their next entrance.

His naturally romantic nature was underpinned by a cool logic. His fantasy, like all good fantasy, was planted firmly in reality. For *The Little Hut*, he reasoned how a sophisticated couple would re-create the trappings of civilized society on a desert island: gourds became pouffes, a seed pod a manicure set, and fantastical tropical fruit cocktail shakers. In *Under the Sycamore Tree* the ants' nest was furnished with a sofa made from a centipede, a wasp-skin rug, a spider chair, and a grasshopper coffee table; the soldier ants' weapons were safety pins and an insecticide spray, while the ant general wore khaki but with red berry pips.

Le Nozze di Figaro *at Glyndebourne, 1955, with Sena Jurinac as the Countess, Sesto Bruscantini as Figaro, and Elena Rizzieri as Susanna. Susanna's eye-catching clear blue dress reflected her clear-headed character rather than her status as a maid.*

Set model for Rashomon, *1959. For director Peter Glenville, Messel's set "consisted of the most magical Japanese forest that actually moved; the trees themselves seemed to come to life."*

Messel's genius as a designer lay not just in his imagination but in how that imagination was realised in theatrical terms. He once said, "I attempted to use every device to make as much magic as possible,"[11] a disingenuous statement which masked the sheer hard work behind every production. Chameleon-like, he absorbed the unique qualities of a script or score, working closely with director or conductor; from these discussions evolved a design style that was a personal but never obtrusive interpretation. Then followed weeks of research into the period, visiting museums and private houses in England and abroad, consulting books, paintings, prints, tapestries, ceramics — soaking up information like blotting paper. Inigo Jones and Jacobean court masques were the obvious starting point for *Comus*, the Fairy Cavaliers and Pages in *The Sleeping Beauty* and *Homage to the Queen*, the Impressionists for

Letter from Paris. The prologue of *The Sleeping Beauty*, with flattened arches and banded columns, derived from Watteau's *Les Charmes de la vie* while Act III drew on soaring Baroque architectural fantasies, and Aurora's Rose Adagio tutu was inspired by Velázquez. A religious procession in Seville, with a Madonna under a canopy, suggested the Queen of the Night's entrance in *Die Zauberflöte*. In Samson, Messel placed the chorus in an arched foreground frame, "as if built for a masque with hedges either side"[12] but which also recalled Diaghilev's 1914 staging of *Le Coq d'or*. For *The Rivals* and *The Country Wife* he painted the props on the scenery, as André Derain did for *La Boutique fantasque*.

Everything was then filtered through his imagination and emerged as pure Messel. The designs looked spontaneous, but they emerged from a long period of trial and error,

Set model for The Lady's Not For
Burning, *1949. Christopher Fry
wrote, "The inventiveness of (the
set) stays in the mind ... the way
to the garden, the feeling of
Spring ... the charm of it, and
particularly the space of sky,
by sunlight, rainlight and
mooonlight ..."*

74 *Messel on Stage*

Set model for Captain Absolute's Lodgings in The Rivals, *1945. Messel often showed interiors and exteriors in his sets, sometimes for practical reasons, but sometimes to suggest a world beyond the immediate stage action.*

75

"whittling and filing, embroidering and confectioning," as Max Beerbohm said of Robert Louis Stevenson. Each production spawned hundreds of preliminary notes, scribbles, and sketches often only intelligible to himself, especially when working on opera: "The music seems to help by forming pictures, elusive as in a dream," he said. "These I try to capture long enough until they can materialize, however vaguely, as a scribble on paper."[13] There were over eight hundred for the Glyndebourne *Die Zauberflöte*.

Once the design crystallised, he built the set models, constructed around a scale figure to ensure perfect proportions, his imaginings translated into plastic, putty, pipe cleaners, matchsticks, snippets of fabric — anything that would convey to the scene builders the exact effect he wanted. He pushed the boundaries. He knew the gossamer weightless conservatory in *Ring Round the Moon* had to be made in metal, only for the scene builders, who traditionally worked in wood, to tell him that it couldn't be done. It

could. In Samson he experimented with projections to give a stylised representation of the destruction of the temple, at once more practical and realistic than collapsing wood and canvas.

Messel's sets were spatially and visually dramatic, environments to be moved *in* and *through*, conceived with groupings, lighting, and stage effects in mind: how to give prominence to a particular character here, how to move large numbers of a chorus there, particularly in essentially static works, like *Samson* or *Idomeneo*. Sets were built up of two-dimensional individual flats, using unusual perspectives and patterns of light and shade, at once architectural and decorative, which confounded the expectations of the proscenium arch stage; rooms and piazzas were slewed at an angle. In *Le Nozze di Figaro* within an angled gazebo wing diagonal arches marched in the opposite direction, setting up a double visual tension. The horror of the gambling scene in *The Queen of Spades* was

intensified by an acutely angled orange table, while the double perspective of the ballroom, peopled with painted figures sinisterly eavesdropping on Lisa and Herman, suggested instability and paranoia.

Practical problems were often solved imaginatively. The park in *The Country Wife*, its single, lonely obelisk and high, narrow arched hedges reminiscent of formal eighteenth-century English gardens, was eerily surreal, but the arches also gave the illusion of height to the Old Vic stage; colonnades in *The Sleeping Beauty* disguised the difficult middle-distance; trompe l'oeil props on the scenery allowed for faster scene changes.

Only when the sets were completed did Messel begin the costumes. "It seems impossible" he said, "for me to do one costume at a time. They all have to be hatched together, like a clutch of eggs."[14] Each design suggested a specific character, its period, stance, and movement: the

cook in *Ariadne auf Naxos*, sophisticated Lady India in *Ring Round the Moon*, Countess Adèle in *Le Comte Ory*, a dozen individual bathers in *Gigi*, ruffians in *Der Rosenkavalier* that Hogarth would not be ashamed to own. In *The School for Scandal*, Snake's unhealthy greenish yellow breeches and dark coat with raised black markings subtly follow through the implications of his name. Messel reworked Baroque heroic theatre costume in several productions, but even within the confines of *Helen!* he differentiated between Paris Menelaus (anachronistically overwhelmed with an ermine cloak) and the pompous thug Achilles.

Final production touches, like costume details, accessories, and props, he found comparatively straightforward, as they followed naturally from the overall concept. His costumes distilled a period or style, although he annoyed purists by mixing periods in *The Sleeping Beauty*; for him,

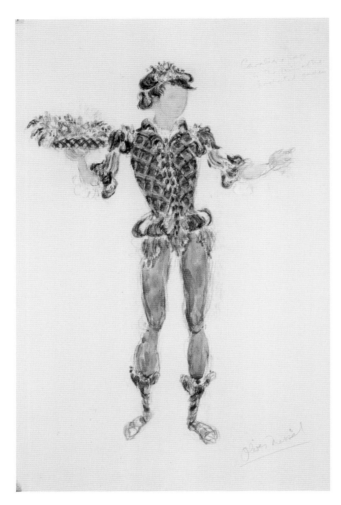

The flavour of seventeenth-century court masque costumes permeates Messel's designs for The Sleeping Beauty, 1946.

Messel understood the different levels of court dress. This costume design is for the Queen for Princess Aurora's birthday, a family yet public celebration held in the palace garden in The Sleeping Beauty, 1946.

FAR RIGHT The Sleeping Beauty, Act III, 1946. Messel's inspiration for the sets were the soaring, majestic fantasies of the Bibienas, most celebrated of Baroque theatrical designers.

the blanket term "eighteenth-century" hid as many variations as the more obvious developments of nineteenth-century fashion. Above all, his costumes were practical, apt, and flattering. His favourite long bodices and "stomacher" panels, which lengthened the torso, were becoming to thin dancer and stout opera singer alike. In *The Queen of Spades*, the Countess's exaggerated, encrusted, ruffled costumes and vast wig overwhelm her, a visualization of her crushing sin, but they also helped diminish the substantial Edith Coates, who sang the role. M. Jourdain's elaborate dressing gown in *Ariadne auf Naxos* immediately said "rich and fussy." Beryl Grey, *The Sleeping Beauty*'s Lilac Fairy in 1946, paid tribute to his understanding of ballet costumes, praising his "gorgeous trimmings that you could dance in — that didn't weigh you down and didn't pull you back when you turned. So often you get dresses that look lovely, but when you move in them — when you turn — they turn after you, stopping your pirouettes."[15] His bold headdresses, of wire, sponge, velvet, and cellophane, which framed without overwhelming the face, were miracles of weightlessness.

As Cochran acknowledged, Messel, unlike many painter-designers, never just created beautiful easel pictures. "He dresses a stage for a play that is to be performed by actors, and he is swiftly and subtly responsive to the dramatic requirements of action and atmosphere."[16] His costumes "played" with or against each other in the constantly shifting groups which mirrored the changing relationships between the characters. His designs were inextricably linked to the overall dramatic scheme and what Cochran said about *The Miracle* was true of any Messel-designed production: "Massine's groupings appeared to be arranged for the effective display of Messel's costumes, while the costumes called aloud for the groupings of Massine."[17] But he equally understood how to create a focal point. In *Helen!*, Evelyn Laye as Helen stood out against all the burlesqued riot in cunningly simple dresses which cleverly married classicism to sleek 1930s style, while the grey tutus of Princess Aurora's friends created a foil for her pink tutu, creating a visual barrier between her and the multicoloured court.

Each design threw up myriad possibilities: How would the sprite in *Zémire et Azor* look? Doglike? Owl-like? What kind of headdress for the Queen of the Waters's *Cavalier in Homage* to the Queen? Shell? Coral? Fish? Seaweed? Sheets were covered with daubs of colour as he worked out the palette for each production. His favourite colours were often characteristic of his time — plum, claret pink, sage green, turquoise, ultramarine, yellow — but he often, unusually, used greys for his heroines, but lifted them with a shot of colour. Equally one bright colour might be married to another. Often, he drew on a specific source: Goya for the dramatic colours of *Il Barbiere de Siviglia*, the jewel-like colours of the *Très riches heures* for *Comte Ory*. He was unafraid of colour: the flash of Don Magnifico's waistcoat in *Cenerentola*, the favourite discord of orange-vermilion and cyclamen pink for Florestan in *The Sleeping Beauty*, Susannah's brilliant yellow in the same scene as the vibrant vermilion of the Countess's dress in act 3 of *Le Nozze di Figaro*, or Fatima's pink dress in *Zémire et Azor*.

The finished drawings were impressions of the costume as seen from the audience. The makers were often daunted but knew that, however nebulous a design seemed, it was possible, and Messel could, if necessary, make it himself. He drew in pencil and watercolour but thought in fabric, cut, draping, and embellishment, and each stroke of the pen or swathe of watercolour evoked the required cut and drape of a material. He understood their differing weights and qualities, how they would take dye, reflect or absorb light, and the alternative ways of realising the decoration. He understood the art of suggestion, that the "real" does not necessarily look real on stage. In his hands the most mundane materials — pipe cleaners, moulded rubber and leather, plastered string, raffia, cut metal, dishcloths, sponge, Christmas tree lights — were transformed. Jewels were chandelier drops backed with sweet papers, or cellophane (which had the advantage of lightness) backed with sequins; moulded and painted chamois leather became embroidery or armour embellishments; Sellotape suggested the gleam of water on costumes in *Homage to the Queen*. Rigid synthetic mesh edged with pipe cleaners became ruffs; it weighted the gauzy trains of the royals in *The Sleeping Beauty*; it encrusted the bodices of the water attendants in *Homage to the Queen* like an exotic fan coral. To create the Queen Ant's throne room in *Under the Sycamore Tree*, he "twisted together 300,000 pieces of felt, 700 feet of wire, and countless gauzes, silks and furry oddments, into a set that seems to vibrate with secret life."[18] Everyone on the production team was in awe of his mastery of all the complex elements of a production, if not his working hours, which usually started just as they were about to go home.

Sketchbooks and storyboards show his concern with every technical detail. A sketchbook sent to director Michael Benthall for *The Queen of Spades* suggests how a nightmare scene should be intensified by lighting, queries

whether he needs to add details for production reasons, and notes what can be entrusted to other experts. The extensive annotations on the *Samson* designs show how his work dovetailed with that of the director, as well as how his concept emerged from the music itself: "As he is led up the steps and reaches behind the archway I imagined some of the Philistines would come dancing down the steps and swirling round him, leaving him horrified and bewildered as he is led through them to the temple. Then the music suggested to me that a dancing procession could whirl in from below prompt side, dancing hand in hand like a long chain, as in revelling scenes at the end of a party."[19]

There was indeed a partylike feeling to Messel's designs, a pleasure in the creative process which communicated itself to the audience. Those who understood the working theatre, like Cochran, James Agate, or Arnold Bennett, called him a genius. Twentieth-century theatre owed him an immeasurable debt, not just for his brilliance, but for raising and consolidating the professional status of the stage designer: during his lifetime, stage design became a discipline and, though he never taught save by example, many of his principles became absorbed into the mainstream. Since Messel died, there have been many great designers, but no one has quite equalled his achievements. He was not a hard act to follow. He was an impossible act to follow.

81

RIGHT *Costume design for* Zerbinetta *in* Ariadne auf Naxos, *Glyndebourne, 1950. Clear yellow was one of Messel's favourite stage colours.*

FAR RIGHT *Costume design for the Ant General in* Under the Sycamore Tree, *1952. Messel wittily suggested the ant's human aspirations by giving the general a standard khaki uniform with his status indicated by berry "pips."*

RIGHT *Dressing gown for M. Jourdain in* Ariadne auf Naxos, *Glyndebourne, 1950. Designers rarely draw the back of a costume, and costume makers usually deduce the back from the front.*

FAR RIGHT *Costume design for a ball dress in* Queen of Spades, *Royal Opera House, 1950. This costume, reminiscent of the folkloric designs of Michel Larionov, is in keeping with the Russian tradition of incorporating folk design into court dress.*

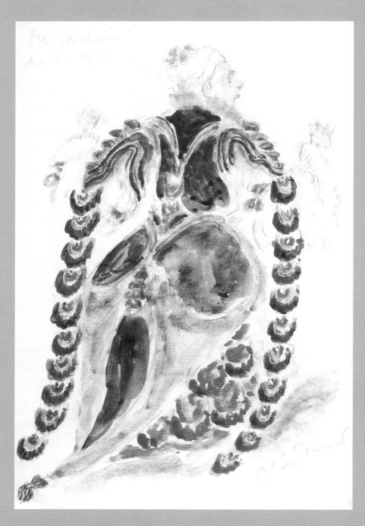

FAR LEFT *A variation on Baroque heroic costume, with hints of medieval armour for Herapha in* Samson *at the Royal Opera House, 1958.*

LEFT *Costume design for Snake in* The School for Scandal, *Copenhagen, 1958.*

FAR LEFT *Costume design for Lisbe in Zémire et Azor, Bath Festival, 1955. Clear colour simply tempered with a swathe of fabric was characteristically Messel.*

LEFT *Costume design for the loutish Achilles in* Helen!, *1932. Messel wittily adapted a Baroque theatre version of Roman military uniform to reflect the individual characters of the Greek heroes.*

Desmond Heeley

Desmond Heeley is a set
and costume designer.

In Ring Round the Moon, *the heroine is described as wearing a dress the colour of smoke. Messel conjured a turn-of-the-century ball gown of transparent silver gauze and grey nets over his favourite saffron yellow, a figure as light and fragile as tissue paper, alone in a moonlit conservatory that was hung with Japanese lanterns, producing an atmosphere of complete and utter magic.*

In New York there was his ominous green bamboo forest for Rashomon *and the gaiety of the musical* The House of Flowers, *where a large blue and white convolvulus became the horn of a gramophone.*

The many caprices: a doll's house to show off a line of paints in House & Garden; *for a wine merchant's Bond Street window, a vine-covered cart with a young Bacchus astride a barrel, being pulled by horses; the Dorchester Hotel in 1953, along the route of the Coronation procession, its exterior covered with wire mesh that held acres of evergreen, the windows draped in scarlet, like boxes at the opera.*

Extraordinary artist, beloved magician of the theatre, a witty, nimble-fingered craftsman, able to delight, instruct, and enchant with ease and charm.

The ways and byways of theatre he knew and contributed to so greatly have all but vanished, but how blessed we are to have so much of his legacy to remind us now and then just how wonderful his incredible world of make-believe once was.

OPPOSITE *One of several rejected designs for the capricious, self-centered Lady India in* Ring Round the Moon, *1950.*

Chapter 4

The Magic of Messel and the Theatre of the Interior

by Jeremy Musson

The drama of the interior: the magnificent bathroom designed and painted in 1937 by Oliver Messel for Wright Ludington at Val Verde, his villa in Santa Barbara, California.

O liver Messel was, at a relatively early age, an internationally acknowledged master of theatre design. He was also admired in his own lifetime for his contribution to the worlds of interior and party decoration, although he is too little recognized for this today. This work encompassed a wide variety of decorative schemes, from murals and richly romantic interiors for hotels, shops, and theatres to his legendary decorations for balls and receptions.[1]

His training as a painter was key to this, and his use of colour and painterly approach to tone was central to everything he did. There was always texture and movement in his colour — it was never flat. It is perhaps difficult to truly separate his interior design work from his stage and film design work, and he may have been more of an influence in the adoption and revival of painting techniques in interior decoration, which we take for granted today, than has been recognised.

It is hardly surprising that he should have applied his inventiveness and his knowledge to other fields of design. Indeed, as quickly as he became famous as a set designer, other people borrowed Messel's ideas for interior work, especially his "all white" or "white on white" sets, for *Helen!* (based on *La Belle Hélène*) in 1932. This certainly directly inspired the work of his friend Syrie Maugham, wife of Somerset, who also happened to be one of London's leading interior decorators.

ABOVE *Oliver Messel, with the looks of a film star, photographed in the Roman bathroom he painted at Val Verde.*

OPPOSITE *The bath was designed to resemble the cistern of a fountain standing amongst the ruins of a Roman palace.*

The Rococo-inspired wedding cake designed by Messel for the wedding of Syrie and Somerset Maugham's daughter Lisa, who married Lt. Col. Vincent Paravicini in 1936.

OPPOSITE *One of the masks by Messel for the decoration of his friend Lord Faringdon's private theatre at Buscot Park, Oxfordshire.*

Cecil Beaton remarked that "with the strength of a typhoon she blew all colour before her. For the next decade Syrie Maugham bleached, pickled or scraped every piece of furniture in sight." She designed interiors for Noël Coward and Stephen Tennant, as well as Fort Belvedere for the Prince of Wales in 1936, and she is also known to have often used decorative paintings by Messel in her interior schemes. Messel also much admired how she "set a scene" as a hostess, and his own awareness of the social choreography of interior space should not be underestimated.[2]

It was apparently not just Syrie who followed in the wake of Messel's visual imagination as expressed on the stage. The art historian James Laver also saw Messel's influence on interiors in the early 1930s when he wrote, "In interior decoration one is constantly struck by the growing number of rooms which are beginning to resemble Messel's studio; white walls, their surface broken by some huge and frankly theatrical moulding, enormous jars suggested by the urns in Italian gardens; a simplicity which is no longer the simplicity of the laboratory, but the stylized simplicity of the good stage set. Colour is given only in the accessories, in the cushions, or in the profusion of flowers. All the rest is white, or 'off white,' a fashion for which Messel, as we have seen has been more responsible than any one."[3]

As with his Slade contemporary and friend Rex Whistler, Messel was an adept muralist. In the 1930s and 1940s, he was called in to provide murals for clubs such as the Bagatelle Club and the San Marco Restaurant (scenes on a Venetian theme) and Fresh Flowers, a flower shop owned by Lady Diana Cooper and Gertrude Lawrence. In the 1950s he was still being commissioned to paint murals at the homes of private individuals such as Billy Wallace in Mayfair and Edgar Ivens at Fairlawne in Kent.[4] Undoubtedly the most significant of his prewar schemes of muralled interior decoration was for a wealthy American art collector, Wright Ludington, who had a large villa in Santa Barbara designed by Bertram Goodhue with gardens and courtyards filled with classical sculpture. In 1937, Ludington commissioned Messel to paint a mural in a bedroom and bathroom suite.[5] The bathroom appears as if in the ruins of a Roman villa, with pillars and stone archways framing painted views of ruined buildings, which seems inspired by the work of Salvador Dalí.[6] The bedroom was designed as a tented room. Messel wrote of its striking colour scheme, "The walls are made like a draped tent of plaster supported on painted garlands. The valence all round of plaster leaves painted with dark green and gold

*In the bathroom at Val Verde,
Messel presented a version of a
ruined Roman palace with a nod
to the surrealism of Salvador Dalí.*

and ornamented with a fringe of golden balls."[7] Where the tent was caught back at the four corners it showed a reveal of bright vermilion, while the curtains of the windows, the walls, and doors were covered with dark green Ottoman silk. The bed was caught up "on dark green spears [and] made of fine broadcloth to look like plaster and lined with dark green silk with lines of fine gold beads." While the tented bedroom does not survive, the bathroom scheme is entirely intact. (Messel was not the only the theatre designer employed, for a blue bedroom was created by set designer Eugene Berman, a Russian-born New Yorker, in his trademark "Berman Blue.")[8]

Messel's talent for theatrical design and improvised effects naturally led him to be in demand for grand party decoration. On the very eve of the Second World War, in August 1939, he was involved in the spectacular costumed ball which was held to raise money for the Georgian Group at Osterley Park, the home of the Earl and Countess of Jersey. The *Architects Journal* described it thus: "In the white and scarlet tent, designed by Oliver Messel, the company danced, countesses and peers, film-stars and socialites…. The band peeped from a frame of bamboo, and wreathed ivy, lights were concealed in sheaves of corn, corner pedestals were crowned with plaster horses' heads, their purple manes tied with green ribbons."[9]

The Second World War certainly presented a dramatic hiatus in Messel's career. He was appointed to the Camouflage Corps, Eastern Command. Messel, with the rank of captain, was posted to Norwich to take charge of the

The tented bedroom at Val Verde
was inspired by a Roman
military camp. The tented bed
was a deep crimson within.

OPPOSITE *The ballroom of the
Assembly House at Norwich
(which Messel chose as the
camouflage factory for Eastern
Command) prepared by Messel
and his fellow officers to hold
a dance.*

The magnificent Royal Box at the Royal Opera House, Covent Garden, decorated with remarkable ingenuity and imagination by Messel for the opening night of Homage to the Queen *in 1953.*

OPPOSITE *Messel's temporary decoration, incorporating antique furniture, for the anteroom of the Royal Box at the Royal Opera House, Covent Garden, during the state visit of the president of France in 1950.*

Eastern Command Camouflage Office. Among Messel's papers are still folders of postcards of ruins and small thatched cottages which appear to be part of his research for his camouflage work.[10] There are also photographs showing mocked-up barns and pigsties for concealing parked military vehicles and artillery and made convincing by the addition of rusted agricultural metalware.

Exploring the old city of Norwich he discovered the eighteenth-century Assembly House being used as a warehouse. As he had been asked find a new base for a camouflage factory, he insisted that the War Office take on the Assembly House for that purpose. He and his fellow officers also held a ball to bring the importance of the rooms to the attention of local grandees. He is still credited there with the structure's rescue.[11]

Messel's camouflage work is mentioned in *The Kitchen Sink*, a memoir by Beverley Nichols, whose butler Sam Gaskin had become Oliver Messel's batman. Nichols recalled a design he was shown on a visit to Norwich: "It was a sketch of a very small iron building, painted pale green with touches of gold, in the mid-Victorian style. It was very delicate and pretty, and at first I took it to be some sort of summer-house, or a band-stand. Not at all, said Oliver; it was intended to be a gentleman's lavatory."[12] That established, Nichols pressed on: "But how would such an object serve the cause of the Allies, I enquired. . . . The Germans would use it, he replied, in the early years of the Invasion. After a protracted voyage across the North Sea they would feel the need of some convenience . . . Therefore when they saw this welcoming little building, standing by the side of the road on one of the main entrances to the city, they would naturally wish to avail themselves of its services. And as soon as they stepped inside it would instantly explode." It never saw action.

The end of hostilities meant that Messel could return fully to the world of theatre and film design. The gilded 1930s was well and truly over, but Messel's stage design career entered a new and highly creative phase. His set designs for the ballet *The Sleeping Beauty* at Covent Garden in 1946 seemed to be a signal that not all of the prewar civilization and glamour had been swept away.[13] Messel also became set and costume designer for the opera theatre at Glyndebourne, newly founded by the Christie family, and designed the proscenium arch there in 1946.[14]

During the early 1950s, Messel was several times asked to supervise the decorations for an expanded Royal Box at Covent Garden. The first, in 1950, was for a command performance in front of the president of France, Vincent

Auriol. This was a masterpiece of theatrical improvisation and is seen as part of the postwar resurgence of the pageantry of the English monarchy. This display required all his talents for invention and inventive reuse of inexpensive materials. His decorations encompassed the elegant foyer, draped and garlanded like a grand tented ballroom, into which Messel introduced gilded antique furniture. He also repainted the walls blue and marbled and gilded the columns.

Messel was eager to make a contribution to the 1951 Festival of Britain celebrations, but seems to have been overlooked in the "brave new world" atmosphere.[15] Messel

had certainly had a private meeting with Sir Gerald Barry, the director of the Festival of Britain, in July 1948, and had suggested a "Tivoli"-styled garden be put on as part of the celebrations. Barry was then planning the role of the Festival Gardens in Battersea Park, and was charmed by Messel's ideas but nervous of their reception elsewhere in his organization.[16] But it may have been Barry who encouraged Messel to produce his extensive proposals, for a grand garden with designs for teahouses and arenas for dancing, ingeniously contrived from trellising.[17]

In 1953 the celebrations surrounding the coronation also led to the second of Messel's defining commissions to

OPPOSITE *For the reception of the president of France in 1950, Messel also redecorated the Crush Bar at the Royal Opera House, Covent Garden, with new paint colours for the walls and marble paint effect on the pilasters.*

ABOVE *A signed and coloured sketch of the blue and white decorative motif for the Crush Bar at the Royal Opera House.*

OPPOSITE *Messel's 1959 set design for the inn in Act III of Mozart's* Der Rosenkavalier *with his characteristic arch within an arch, all framed within his Glyndebourne proscenium arch.*

In 1946, Messel redesigned the proscenium arch of the theatre at Glyndebourne in a baroque style. For many years after that he would be the leading set designer for the Glyndebourne Opera.

dress the Royal Box at Covent Garden, this time for the Gala performance of Malcolm Arnold's *Homage to the Queen*.[18] As the *Illustrated London News* described it, on June 13, 1953, "The glittering transformation scene in the auditorium at Covent Garden tonight was the work of Mr. Oliver Messel, much of it achieved by a gigantic 'make do and mend' effort carried out by his own hands. Mr. Messel sat up for three nights making oak leaves out of sticky brown paper painted green and gold, and Royal ciphers out of wire with folds of ribbon."[19]

In the following year he decorated the Royal Box for the state visit of the king of Sweden. Messel also worked on the decoration of a ball given by Lady Marriott, which *Vogue* magazine described simply as "the most beautiful party London has seen in years."[20] He also designed the wedding party for Sir Berkeley Ormerod, at the Dorchester Hotel. In 1960, he designed a ball for the American ambassador Jock Whitney with elaborate water-gardens inspired by Versailles.[21]

Also in 1953 and also at the Dorchester, Messel received a commission to furnish a suite of rooms on the seventh floor of a newly built extension.[22] Messel designed the much-admired temporary decoration, suggestive of the tiered boxes of an opera house, on the front of the hotel overlooking the route of the coronation procession.[23]

The same luxurious romanticism was applied to the interiors of the suite, now known as the Messel Suite.[24] The entrance hall and lobby have a distinctly Regency character and lead to the large drawing room, which has an evocative English garden theme; the specially woven carpet had a suggested parterre pattern, slightly abstracted into swathes of green, brown, and pink. The latticework framing the door and a large painting are actually interwoven painted lead casings then used on electrical wiring, an example of Messel's famous "make do and mend" philosophy. Building materials were still scarce after the war, and his assistants on this scheme, John Claridge and Carl Toms, were constantly sent out to improvise materials.[25] The bedroom is richly coloured in warm yellows, with a bed canopy in an imperial Chinese yellow Ottoman fabric. The bathroom not only has mirrors decorated with chinoiserie paintings by Messel but an extraordinary gilded lavatory seat in Venetian Rococo style — once seen, never forgotten.

The hotel management and guests responded well to the fantastical yet deeply comfortable atmosphere. Messel was almost immediately commissioned to provide a related series of rooms for entertaining, firstly the Penthouse

A detail of the vaulted lobby in the Messel Suite of the Dorchester Hotel, London, which Messel decorated in 1953.

dining room, added in 1954 on the ninth floor, and then in 1956 the Pavilion Room, for drinks, parties, and receptions.[26]

The dining room was conceived as a fantastical mirrored space, with interlaced oak branches and leaves in blue and gold plasterwork, inspired by his designs for the enchanted forest in *The Sleeping Beauty*. The curtains are a red carmine silk. The Pavilion was in an overtly Regency-inspired scheme, in which he employed Etruscan detailing associated with his designs for *The Magic Flute*. All these rooms were restored in the 1990s.[27]

In 1954, Messel redesigned the venerable premises of Justerini and Brooks on Bond Street,[28] which became a masterful series of again Regency-inspired rooms with detailing echoing his work at the Dorchester. *The Daily Express* observed of the dramatic changes, "Customers sail in through doors of Regency prettiness and on into the sale-rooms where the carpets are colored the delicate shade of just-pressed grape-juice, where the walls are hung in claret velvet. Wine is tasted in little rooms with white chandeliers … And everywhere is shimmering glass set in carved white woodwork like sugar icing." It sounds good enough to eat. One of the firm's partners, Ralph Cobbold, said, "We had to curb Oliver in expense a bit. You know he would dash in and say 'I've found the cheapest line in gold door knobs — only £50 apiece.' We had to break it to him that we could only run to brass."[29]

In 1957, while he was busy with designs for a series of theatrical productions, he was also asked to redesign the Paris headquarters of *Reader's Digest* (it is not known how much was executed) then situated on 216, Boulevard Saint Germain. In this same year he designed a new boardroom for the Messel family's brokerage firm.[30]

The following year he was commissioned by Nicky Sekers to design a small theatre for recitals, concerts, and plays.[31] Sekers had come to Britain in the 1930s and set up the highly successful West Cumberland Silk Mills (also known as Sekers Silks) in Whitehaven. Sekers, who knew Messel through Glyndebourne, wanted to create a theatre

A photograph of Messel showing the scale model of the interiors of the suite he designed for the Dorchester Hotel overlooking Hyde Park. The coloured inset shows the same model now in the Victorian and Albert Museum's collection.

OPPOSITE *The Messel Suite was designed as a celebration of the English garden with a specially designed chintz and a carpet woven to Messel's design in the style of a parterre.*

FOLLOWING PAGES
Messel himself painted the door panels and the framed painting of a garden in the early eighteenth-century style.

at his home, Rosehill, in Cumberland. Sekers had acquired fittings from the Royal Standard, the old musical hall in Whitehaven, although only a small fraction of these were eventually used. Messel and local architect Ronald Gray created an intimate auditorium lined in red silk. Messel designed the proscenium arch and a series of miniature faux boxes, which give the small interior a festive air. The stylish foyer and entrance hall were hung in green silk; the bar was lined with gold brocade specially designed for Rosehill. The theater opened in September 1959 and continues in operation today. Messel himself wrote, "All the decorations for the Rosehill Theatre have been completed within six weeks, the candelabras, proscenium seating and everything." John Claridge, Messel's former assistant, had joined Sekers and was seconded to help realize Messel's designs.[32]

The gilded lavatory seat was designed on the model of Venetian Rococo seat furniture and is a typical Messel detail, as is the Venetian Rococo–style painting of a figure on the mirror glass.

The Naples yellow border for the curtains, with two green oak leafs, was specially designed by Messel for the suite he designed at the Dorchester, and he used this motif elsewhere.

OPPOSITE Looking into the master bedroom of the Messel Suite with its walls hung in a warm yellow silk with an oak-leaf border.

FOLLOWING PAGES
The master bedroom of the Messel Suite. Faithfully restored in the 1990s, it preserves the colour and verve of a typical Messel interior scheme.

The figure of the Bacchus modeled by Messel for the penthouse dining room he designed for the Dorchester Hotel in 1954.

OPPOSITE *The breathtaking mirrored dining room was designed to appear like a scene from the Enchanted Forest in the ballet* The Sleeping Beauty.

FOLLOWING PAGES
The Pavilion Room, another entertainment room, designed in 1956 by Messel for the Dorchester Hotel in a more distinctively Regency Revival style.

Messel's work in New York was more fraught but was celebrated in the press. Billy Rose, lyricist and impresario, asked Messel to redesign the 1920s National Theatre in New York. Messel wrote in August 1959, "The whole building is, of course, designed expressly to create the atmosphere of a theatre of the 18th-century tradition, done in my own way."[33] One the eve of the opening in September 1959, in *The Theatre* magazine Messel related how the project was conducted and how, with reference to a carefully scaled model, he spent several weeks "making hundreds of drawings covering every phase of the called-for detail, from the décor and color on the gold seeming proscenium arch to the precise size, nature and individual

Japanese silk paper, the other with a green Thai silk, and the Octagon room in between in yellow. Messel felt these contrasts created both a sensation of richness and a desire to move from one room to the other, to look round the corner. Messel united two shop-fronts: "Decorative ironwork balconies have been designed to bridge the different window levels and link the buildings into one. The treatment of the new facade is intended to retain the forms traditional to regency London and suitable to Old Bond Street." Inside, Messel wrote, "The entrance lobbies are made like ornamental arcades with showcases and mirrors used to give the impression of increased space. . . . All the borders are painted by hand with leaves and flowers, and the embellishments are of burnished gold."[35]

One visitor to Rayne's, Phyllis Watkins, was so dazzled with the interiors that she asked Messel to design the interiors of her own house in Gloucestershire, Flaxley Abbey. This was a decade-long association during which Messel redesigned the entire interior of an English country house with a sense of theatricality, subtlety, and taste.[36]

Mrs. Watkins had complete faith in Messel's taste, and much of his work survives. The old house was picturesque, but dark and inconvenient. The drama of Messel's interior design begins at the entrance hall, with the murals of landscapes painted by his own hand filling two arches, facing two mirrored arches. Messel also inserted two theatrical lights which appear to bathe the landscapes in moonlight.

The Morning Room is hung in patterned gold damask, with bookcases in the Regency manner on either side of the chimneypiece; the windows are draped in gold damask curtains. The carpet was specially woven in Naples for the room. Messel transformed the dining room by opening up two dummy windows. He also painted the walls a pale peach, based on a colour shown in the original eighteenth-century drawing.[37]

The ground-floor Bow Drawing Room was entirely Messel's creation out of a series of small rooms; as James Lees-

placement of each lighting fixture." The exterior décor was composed of greys, off-whites, and a red-and-gold marquee over the entrance, while interior décor was done in a deep red, with gold and white accents. Little survives today, although the theatre still stands.

Messel's most widely remembered British commercial interior design commission after the Dorchester hotel was for Edward Rayne, who engaged him to design a shoe salon on Old Bond Street. In 1959, Rayne wrote that it was "the prettiest shoe-salon in the world, a lighthearted fantasy in white, gold and iridescent silks."[34] Each room was like a jewel box. One was lined with a damson-coloured

Milne wrote in *Country Life* in 1973, "The pearl stippled walls are a sober background to the rose coral silk curtains of the windows in the bow and along the south wall." Messel also introduced a screen of Corinthian columns at one end and mid-eighteenth-century doorcases.

He created an especially elegant bedroom for Mrs. Watkins, in which "he hung the walls with blue silk specially woven, the borders finished with braid." The curtains were glazed chintz made from French blocks, while the bed canopy was unpatterned and "of deep sea blue and cream." Messel also introduced a new passage to serve the seventeenth-century bedrooms which face west and he

treated the woodwork with "a complicated treatment of blow lamps, wire brushes and dragging over gesso" which then assumed "the grey patina of faded paintwork of the 17th century." For these bedrooms, he designed a patterned fabric called Cluny. James Lees-Milne told the owner that "it is very difficult to justice to the house as it is so beautiful."[38]

From 1961 to 1963 Messel was involved in the restoration of the Bath Assembly Rooms (he had also advised on the York Assembly Rooms).[39] The huge Georgian assembly rooms at Bath had been damaged by bombing in 1942, indeed left as a roofless shell. They were eventually

A sketch proposal by Messel for a tea pavilion (unexecuted) for the Festival of Britain. This was proposed as part of the Festival Gardens on Battersea Park, for which Messel wanted to revive the spirit of the famous eighteenth-century Vauxhall Gardens.

ABOVE *The magical interiors designed by Messel for Rayne's Shoe Shop on Old Bond Street, in London, 1959. It was described by his patron as "a lighthearted fantasy in iridescent silks."*

RIGHT *The octagonal anteroom in Rayne's Shoe Shop; Messel designed each room to be like a little jewel box.*

ABOVE *A vaulted and mirrored showroom in Rayne's Shoe Shop, with showcases in the manner of library bookcases.*

LEFT *The main showroom at Rayne's Shoe Shop was hung with a damson-coloured Japanese silk paper. The recesses hung with chintz have the feel of bay window seats in a country house, and the arches echo a triumphal arch.*

Flaxley Abbey, Gloucestershire. Messel was called in to decorate the interiors of this romantic country house by Phyllis Watkins, who had encountered his work first in Rayne's Shoe Shop.

FOLLOWING PAGES
The entrance hall at Flaxley Abbey. Messel's mural painting of a grandly scaled Italianate urn seen against a landscape background was always to be illuminated with a stage light, creating an almost moonlit look.

Flaxley Abbey, looking through a jib-door in the bookcase into the morning room, hung with a gold-coloured silk damask and late Georgian-style curtain arrangements devised by Messel.

OPPOSITE *The morning room, with curtains, carpet, chimneypiece, and bookshelves all designed by Messel.*

FOLLOWING PAGES
PAGES 126–27 *The dining room at Flaxley Abbey, still in its original peach-coloured paintwork, with the curtains designed by Messel and the painted dining room chairs he designed for the room.*

PAGES 128–29 *One of the older bedrooms in Flaxley Abbey for which Messel designed the bed and hung it in a textile called Cluny, which he developed especially for use in the older rooms of the house.*

Messel was much in demand to design lighthearted temporary decorations for balls and dances, often executed in painted trelliswork.

restored to their original proportions in 1956 by Sir Albert Richardson. With a meagre budget of little over £4,000, Messel skillfully devised a pale blue and Naples yellow colour scheme. He had girandole mirrors copied in fibreglass and gilded. Messel's colour scheme was superseded with a new scheme by David Mlinaric, which was influenced by the rooms' original colours.[40]

Evidence of Messel's ability to resolve problems in an existing historic context is given by his work in an important Sussex house: In 1962 Messel was asked to design the decoration of the ceiling of the Long Gallery at Parham for Clive Pearson.[41] His daughter, Veronica Tritton, recalled that they had spent decades restoring the house and had left the Long Gallery to last. Her father said it should be something new: "Let what we do be this generation's contribution to the old house ... It need not be hideous just because it is modern." Messel ingeniously changed the Victorian three-section ceiling into one of five sections and

OPPOSITE *The main saleroom
for Berry Brothers in Messel's
Regency Revival style. The carpet
colour was described as "just-
pressed grape juice, where the
walls are hung in claret velvet."
Note the echo of a triumphal arch
behind the desk.*

The spirit of a designer is often vividly expressed in his own home, and for many years Messel's home was at Pelham Place in Kensington, his place of work and entertainment.[43] In 1960 a journalist for *Today* magazine described it thus: "Strangers tend to reel a bit on entering. For the house is fantastic, a luxuriously decorated, eye-beguiling jewel-box of a place. Everywhere there is magnificence: Aubusson carpets; drapes in mustard and crimson; pillars; arches; pedestals; chaise-longues; pictures, plaques, wall-lamps, model theatre sets, luster's; and in every corner, mounds of spring flowers, sparkling, scintillating."[44]

When his dining room with its lavish place settings was published in *Vogue* in 1963, it was described as "a creative mélange of decorative furnishings of several persuasions brought together through his personal artistry. The molten greens and gold are sharpened by white Indian lawn curtains and a white organdie table cloth … The table is ringed by white-painted Regency chairs."[45] His home in Barbados from 1964 will be considered in the next chapter.

Messel's interior design work must be seen in the context of his time; it must be stressed that these were always (until he started to design new houses in the West Indies) essentially excursions from his principal work for the theatre, ballet, and especially opera. Messel's interior design is strongly influenced by those worlds, in colour and paint technique and his intense interest in art history. His set and costume designs were deeply imbued with the eighteenth century, but the commercial and domestic interiors he worked on have a distinctly Regency character. If Messel's interior work might be gathered under one useful heading, it could be Osbert Lancaster's "Vogue Regency."[46] Lancaster described this as essentially "twentieth-century Transitional." If anyone rode this "Transitional'" era with an irrepressible sense of vibrant colour, spatial invention, theatre, and just sheer fun, it was surely Oliver Messel.

*Messel created a typically
engaging vista within Justerini
and Brooks on Old Bond Street,
with his trademark Regency
Revival fanlights over the doors.*

he raised it by nearly a foot. Wandering branches of foliage are painted on squares of canvas, and timber ribs hide the joins. The whole ceiling had to be dismantled and rebuilt so that it was only finally installed in 1967. Veronica Tritton wrote to Messel in December of that year: "How we have been wishing that you were with us to share the excitement of watching your flowering trees growing slowly down the length of the Long Gallery."[42]

Main stairway could circle down to small foyer
double swing doors on left lead directly into stalls
Foyer curtained opening or folding doors on right lead into the Stalls Bar
above under stairway with banquette settees   three dimensional theatre model
                                                decoration above it.

*Two of Messel's imaginative
designs for the main stairway
from the foyer and stalls bar for
the Billy Rose Theatre in New
York, in 1959. The whole theatre
was, Messel argued, done in an
eighteenth-century style "in my
own way."*

OPPOSITE BELOW *The silk-lined
theatre at Rosehill, Whitehaven,
which Messel designed for Sir
Nicholas (Nikki) Sekers and
which opened in 1959. The faux
boxes originally concealed stage
lighting.*

Stalls bar. bar mainly contained in cellar portion below street. but forming a bay out into the room. decorative ballustrade work on the face of the Bar far door left into service store Room.
another door near left. balancing. leads to Ladies Powder Room etc.

ABOVE *Messel's own dining room in his house in Pelham Place, South Kensington, in 1963, decorated in his most extravagant manner and described in Vogue as "a creative mélange of decorative furnishings."*

RIGHT *The Long Gallery at Parham House, Sussex, where in the 1960s Messel was asked to redesign the ceiling and paint the trailing branches which evoke Elizabethan and Jacobean plasterwork.*

OPPOSITE *The elegant Rococo-style monkey painted on the wardrobe in the master bedroom in the Messel Suite in the Dorchester Hotel was a typically lighthearted Messel motif.*

ABOVE *The "Messel Room" at Old House near Nymans, Sussex, the former country retreat of Messel's nephew the Earl of Snowdon, with typical Messel elements: chintz curtains, faceted mirror, and chinoiserie small table all to Messel's own design.*

FOLLOWING PAGES *The overdoor to Lord Snowdon's Kensington home, intended as a homage to the delicate details so beloved of Messel.*

Nicky Haslam

Nicky Haslam is an interior designer and writer.

The stylish taste in decoration for much of the 1920s was still the vibrant poppy reds, oranges, and blacks, lacquered and low-cushioned, perfumed with Guerlain's Mitsouko. But toward the end of the decade the taste and the palette was to change irrevocably.

In the vanguard creating this romantic movement were three leading members of the Bright Young People, that set which, for all its somewhat self-conscious larking, produced some brilliant poets, writers, and artists. Of the latter, among the more stellar were Cecil Beaton, who eventually concentrated on photography, and the supreme draughtsman Rex Whistler, but the most dazzling, both in looks and talent, was Oliver Messel.

Oliver Messel's work as an interior decorator was inventive, subtle, elegant, and scholarly. Those incomparable qualities are his memorial; that added dash of iridescent lightheartedness is his unique legacy.

OPPOSITE *Messel photographed by Edward Mandinian, in his own home in Pelham Place, South Kensington, which was described by one journalist as "an eye-beguiling jewel-box of a place.*

Chapter 5

Messel as Interpreter of the Caribbean Palladian Style

by Jeremy Musson

B efore Oliver Messel, no stage designer had become so involved in architecture since Inigo Jones. After a full and varied career in theatre design, Messel was the designer and de facto architect of a remarkable series of simple but elegant houses in exotic locations. Beginning in 1964, he remodelled or built nine houses close to the fashionable beaches on the west coast of Barbados, and, from 1969, on the resort island resort of Mustique, he built a further seventeen.[1]

These houses demonstrate his extraordinary gift of visualization into three dimensions, his sense of the choreography of the domestic space, and his real genius for linking house, garden, and landscape through vista, axis, and lighting effect. There was always a playfulness too — which he once articulated as creating "the suggestion of an even grander palace around the corner" — inspired by his experience of the garden of Harold Acton's villa, La Pietra. Indeed, echoes of the mellow farmhouses and palaces of his beloved Italy can be found in many of his works.[2]

Bizarrely, Messel came to his architectural role almost by accident. By the early 1960s, arthritis led him to spend increasing amounts of time in the West Indies, especially Barbados. He and his partner, Vagn Riis-Hansen, bought a house in 1964, and (after a hip operation) in 1966 he took the decision to live full time in Barbados. They first went to Barbados in the late 1950s as guests of architect and developer Victor Marson.

Messel's model for the butterfly-plan house commissioned by Sidney Bernstein to build on the west coast of Barbados, which was not executed.

Most of the English and North American visitors to Barbados in the 1950s and 1960s were well-heeled. Sir Edward Cunard had bought the Glitter Bay Hotel in the 1930s, and Ronald Tree had built the Sandy Lane Hotel after the war, helping to make the west coast of Barbados fashionable. In 1947, Tree had built himself a new home right on the Sandy Lane beach: a grand Palladian villa designed by Geoffrey Jellicoe, and modelled on Palladio's Villa di Maser.[3]

One of the Sandy Lane plots was sold by Tree to Sir Sidney (later Lord) Bernstein. He approached Messel around 1963 to design a house there.[4] An architectural model was made showing a deceptively simple two-storey villa with side wings, glimpsed through palm trees, with shady balconies of trelliswork. However, it was never built, and Bernstein eventually took on a different architect. By this time Messel had become involved in the remodelling of

Leamington House, a little farther up the coast, for Drue and Jack Heinz; he also built for them the classical single-storey, H-plan Leamington Pavilion, completed in January 1964. Messel by now also had begun to think of building himself a house in Barbados.[5]

So in the summer of 1964, Messel and Riis-Haagen bought a near derelict, eighteenth-century seafront plantation house on the seafront, named Maddox, which Messel redesigned and remodelled to make a comfortable and elegant home.[6] The house, finished by early 1965, immediately caught the imagination of many visitors, some of whom approached him to design or help remodel other houses on the island.

Although Messel's relationships with clients and builders alike could be tempestuous, the resulting houses are all works of art, testaments to his artistry and imagination. Messel himself considered that he had had "wonder-

ful luck, marvelous opportunities in designing buildings and things which any ordinary architect would give their eyes to have [had]."[7]

What was key to Messel's success as an "amateur" architect was his ability to design houses which drew on the Georgian plantation house tradition and at the same time could frame an entirely modern type of what he called "indoor-outdoor living" — Charles Graves aptly described Messel's style as "Caribbean Palladian." Messel's own social and artistic background and his "eye" as a theatre designer all contributed to the almost innate sense of scene setting and architectural proportion that he exercised in the design of these buildings.[8]

His style is symbolized by the repeated motif of the broad Regency-style elliptical arch which appears in several of his houses. This also seems to owe something to the proportions of the proscenium arch of a theatre; and these

PREVIOUS PAGES
LEFT *The colonnade at Maddox, with his characteristic Doric columns, cast in a mould, in concrete mixed with coral-stone dust.*

RIGHT *The comfortable "indoor-outdoor" spirit of Maddox included this elegant open sitting loggia with views across a garden to the sea, as photographed in 1979.*

OPPOSITE *The dining loggia, with the pineapple side table, designed by Messel, characteristic of his inventive approach to furniture design.*

arches naturally frame the view out toward the sea or garden, but also frame the view back into the house itself and reveal the life inside as if on a stage, especially if looking in from the beach or garden at night.

When in a recorded interview, Messel's nephew Lord Snowdon pressed him on his attitude toward modernism, Messel replied simply: "I don't like to divorce myself from what I find is beautiful . . . I think it was good being in the army, and being [in] camouflage. Because I think it is rather tiresome if a house is too conspicuous; I rather like it melting in. That's why I criticize a lot of modern architecture . . .[that it is] exhibitionist." He also referred in this conversation to wanting to make a house "like a bird's nest."[9]

For a designer such as Messel, every detail counted toward the image he was creating. He paid the most exacting attention not only to the textures of the coral stone, but also of the cement mixed with coral stone, which he used for columns and stucco, as well as to natural and painted timber details. Messel effectively ran a workshop from his garage, run by Carl Chandler, his assistant on many of his building projects. He also collaborated with a stonemason and carver called Mr. Massiah for thirteen years and with

PREVIOUS PAGES
The guest cottage at Maddox, designed to read as almost a folly among the palm trees, has hosted royalty during Messel's ownership of Maddox in the form of Prince Charles.

OPPOSITE *The verdant and atmospheric courtyard at Maddox. Messel cared a great deal about the right planting for his courtyards and took great pains with the plantings of gardens.*

FOLLOWING PAGES
ABOVE LEFT *Crystal Springs, Barbados, next door to Maddox, is an older house which Messel remodelled in 1966, including the addition of the Doric colonnade.*

BELOW LEFT *The archway frames a view through the house straight through to the sea; the house has an open dining loggia with fountain overlooking the beach.*

RIGHT *The Doric colonnade at Crystal Springs frames a series of Messel's trademark round-arched and shuttered casement windows.*

master craftsman Mr. Walcott, who produced mahogany furniture. His chief builders were Arlen Broome and Randolph Cadogan.[10]

Messel also devised many inexpensive building techniques such as simple cement floors lined out and painted to look like glazed earthenware tiles. Elsewhere he used unpromising elements such as the ridged rods used in concrete constructions as decorative balusters for an external staircase.

Messel's interest in the interiors of these houses was intense. He deferred to the local climate, which was radically different from that in England, although familiar contrivances such as arches and light neoclassical detailing helped bridge the two worlds. He collaborated with other decorators on the island such as Robert Thompson and Heather Aguilar. He also developed his trademark pale sage green for shutters, woodwork, iron furniture, and floors alike, and which has become known as "Messel Green" or sometimes "Mustique Green," as also used on many of the new houses on that island.[11] Messel designed both wooden and ironwork furniture that could be made on the island by local Barbadian craftsmen, working under his supervision, with simple variations on traditional themes: simplified eighteenth-century here, Regency chi-

noiserie there. His principal metalworking craftsman was a Mr. Sandiford.[12]

Some of his surviving designs show in plan an interest in what might be called the "social choreography" of these houses, hardly surprising in one so identified with the design and dressing of elite social events in London.[13] Sketches show how he thought through how the furniture would be used (for instance, where tables for bridge might be placed), and how loggias, verandas, and garden buildings contributed to private entertainment.

Messel's own house at Maddox exemplifies his inventive approach to a "villa" dwelling in the classical sense. It began with one eighteenth-century stone building, which was oriented with a side wall facing the sea, in the manner of many older houses on the island. Messel reoriented the house and wrote: "While anxious to retain the thick walls and all the character of the old house, I have attempted to reconstruct the building to suit our way of living in the tropics. By the additions, the house has been turned so that the open loggias and sitting areas now all have the full advantage of the sea."[14]

The house is approached through a cool colonnaded courtyard, with trees and a fountain, leading to the living and dining rooms, which are both loggias open to the

Leamington Pavilion, Barbados, right on the beach, was designed by Messel as a guest house. The colonnade was extended and the pool created at a later date.

FOLLOWING PAGES
PAGES 162–63 *Mango Bay,
Barbados, was the only complete
new building on the island
designed by Messel, but nonetheless
it makes use of many traditional
Barbadian details including the
distinctive "jalousied" shutters. It
was completed in 1969.*

PAGES 164–65 *The deep double-
storey verandas and balconies
of Mango Bay were inspired by
traditional planter's houses of
the West Indies and the American
Deep South.*

garden. The Doric columns were cast from a carved mould in a mixture of cement and the dust of coral stone.

While the views to the sea were paramount, Messel valued the mature trees which framed the views, which gave the garden character and shape, characteristics that he augmented with plants and terraces and walkways. He also went to elaborate lengths to protect older trees on every building plot on which he worked. With his gardener (later butler) Johnson, he planted frangipani, chalice vines, hibiscus: "The garden I have approached purely as painting a picture, not collecting plants for their rarity but to form a composition with the pattern and colours of the leaves and flowers. A controlled Rousseau jungle."

One is reminded of Sir Roy Strong's observation about Messel's ballet sets in the late 1940s and 1950s: "They had grandeur expressed through a silvery transparency of effect as though one were wandering through a dream."[15] The same air of the garden as a kind of dream landscape can still be felt in some of Messel's Barbados houses, at Maddox and at Fustic House in particular, where Messel was an early adopter of electric up-lighters in the gardens.

Messel supervised craftsmen and builders closely to achieve the results he wanted. He often had walls and columns pulled down to be rebuilt, with remarks to his builders like that overheard by his friend Nick Parravacino in Barbados: "That's wonderful, darling, but I think we are going to have to pull it all down and start again"; or as Brian Alexander, manager of the Mustique Land Company, recalled hearing Messel saying on Mustique to a builder creating one of those trademark Messel arches: "No, flatter, it must be flatter."[16]

The garden front of Cockade repeats the triangular pediment of the entrance front. The steps and terracing theatrically extend the social space of the house.

But perhaps this process of detailed supervision and continual attention was the source of the houses' ageless feel and contributed to their handcrafted texture, which sets them radically apart from so much being built in the modernist spirit of the 1960s. Messel was also noted for his ability to make his buildings look as if they were older and more settled than they were, for instance by encouraging moss to grow on the stone.

His regular Barbadian builder, Arlen Broom, recalled, "Mr. Messel was more of a designer in his approach to architecture than an actually qualified architect. He tended to work from imagination — and the next day he would change his mind and the work he had told me to do."[17] But the results worked. As in his theatre work, Messel usually dedicated himself to considerable research of photographs, engravings, and prints for reference.

In 1966, Messel was brought in by Jock Cottell to remodel the house at Crystal Springs, which he did in an ingenious design that has the air of a small Italian villa. The house, which stands just next door to Maddox and is only some five metres above beach level is screened by a narrow but shade-giving Doric colonnade.[18] The elliptical arches of the dining loggia look directly out through the trees to the sea. The same year, he also worked on nearby Alan Bay (now demolished), which looked directly onto the picturesque Sandy Lane Beach, for Peter Moores, son and heir to the football pools fortune. This was an adapation of an existing house with Messel's improvements including the verandah overlooking the sea and the redesign of the dining room as well as work on the garden.[19]

The open central loggia at
Cockade used for both sitting
room and dining room
exemplifies Messel's "indoor-
outdoor living" approach to
the design.

In 1968 Messel worked for Sir Roderick Brinkman at St. Helena, in the parish of St. James, to remodel the staircase and add a double-storey bow with Regency-style verandahs. In the same year, he also designed a new dining room and living room for Queen's Fort, a house on the edge of the Heron Bay estate for Mr. and Mrs. Bill Packard. These were to be added to either side of an existing single-storey house, built in the 1930s. Only the dining loggia was completed.[20]

One of Messel's most extensive remodelling projects of an older house, after his own at Maddox, was Fustic House, in the parish of St. Lucy, a deliciously wooded area with mature mahogany trees some two hundred metres from the sea. There was an existing older stone-built plantation house here, dating back to the eighteenth century. Messel may have known the house when it was owned by Englishwoman, Charmian Fane, who grew orchids commercially there.[21] In 1968, Miss Fane sold the house to Vivien Graves, and Messel transformed the house with considerable imagination and flair for her and her husband, Charles Graves, the writer and brother of the poet Robert Graves. Surviving letters show a considerable rapport between Mrs. Graves and Messel: for her, he created one of his masterpieces. He added a two-storey guest wing with an arcaded sitting loggia with terracing views through trees out to the sea, and he created the remarkable lagoon pool. Vivien Graves's letters record complete delight with his designs and her confidence that the result would be a "tearing beauty."[22] Fustic House was completed in 1969. Patricia Forde, who visited the house with Messel during the work there, felt that "Oliver was always at peace here . . . he always had ideas about what else could be done here."[23]

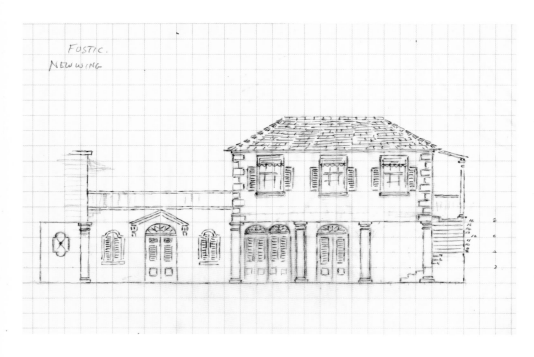

Messel's design for a new wing
for Fustic House, Barbados, an
eighteenth-century planter's
house which he remodelled for
Vivien and Charles Graves.

RIGHT *Messel's wing added
to the north end of the old
plantation house, in a sensitive
classical style, with many
traditional Barbadian details.
The staircase wraps around
the outside of the building
in traditional style.*

The south front of Fustic House, with the shaped gable, reminiscent of Cape Dutch architecture, and terrace and fountain all designed by Messel.

Messel clearly played a role in the landscaping here, most importantly creating the stylish, natural-seeming swimming pool out of the rock. Fustic House is considered one of the best-preserved of the Messel houses on the island and still possesses that otheworldliness that Messel aimed to create.

Mango Bay is the only completely newly built house by Messel on Barbados. Messel had first bought this land close to the beach with a view to building himself a new house for himself, but, unable to afford this, he was eventually persuaded to sell the property to a Sally Aall, on condition that he could design the house that was to be built on the plot.[24] The design executed in 1968 and 1969 shows how much Messel cared about the indigenous character of Barbadian architecture. Despite his trademark open loggias and balconies, he still contrived to manipulate the whole to appear of appropriate scale and to be part of the Georgian classical tradition that defines so much of the historic architecture of Barbados.

One of his other much-admired houses, completed about 1974, was Cockade, for Polly, who was from an old Barbadian landowning family, and who knew Messel socially through Ronald Tree. She and her boyfriend Derek Grewcock purchased a house that had itself been built on the site of a seventeenth-century plantation house.[25] Messel reduced this to a mere shell, raised the ceilings in every room, laid his hallmark scored-concrete floors, and created an open sitting loggia (also used for dining) in the

The atmospheric courtyard formed between the old house and the new wing designed by Messel at Fustic House.

The open sitting loggia, designed by Messel with his typical broad and flattened arch, which framed the views out to the sea that he felt were so important to the enjoyment of these houses.

The lagoon pool at Fustic House, designed by Messel to appear as a natural pool in a clearing, was created by blasting out rock.

One of Messel's designs for a pergola as part of the redevelopment of the old Queen's Park garrison buildings in Bridgetown, Barbados, to provide a new theatre, museum, and public space.

OPPOSITE *Messel designed a number of oriental-style garden pavilions and bandstands, including this one for the garden of Government House.*

FOLLOWING PAGES
The Cotton House Hotel, Mustique, built in 1969–70, with its distinctive open verandah, still plays a central role in the social life of the island. The associated pool originally included a large ruined folly.

centre of the west front, a library to the north, and a master bedroom and smaller sitting room to the south. The master bedroom opened out directly toward an enclosed garden, which he helped create and which terminated in a view of three ruined arches created by Messel as a folly. Cockade is in some ways the most overtly eighteenth-century of the houses designed by Messel, with triangular pediments on both main elevations.[26]

Messel was also interested in contributing to more public-minded projects in Barbados. Queen's Park Theatre was largely made according to his designs but not under his supervision, and his proposals for various museum buildings were never executed. However, he did design gazebos for Government House and for the British high commissioner's house, both of which survive, and he also advised on interior presentation and picture hanging in Government House.[27]

By chance another opportunity arose at almost the same time to help shape the destiny of a whole West Indian island, Mustique, one of the smaller of the Grenadines. At sixty-five, the age when many Englishmen considered themselves ready to retire, Messel took on a formidable role there. Messel's work began directly at the invitation of Colin Tennant (later Lord Glenconner),[28] who knew Messel through Princess Margaret — the wife of Messel's nephew Antony Armstrong-Jones (who became the Earl of Snowdon). By her own account, Princess Margaret considered Messel a beloved uncle figure and stayed with him often in Barbados. Tennant, whose wife, Lady Anne, was lady-in-waiting to the princess, gave Princess Margaret a plot of land on Mustique as a wedding present in 1960 and promised to build her a modest villa there at his own expense. Messel was nominated as the architect and designed for her a simple cottage-like house, almost a collection of pavilions, with a strong axial line from the entrance through a classic Messel arch, and on to the sea, with rooms either side.[29] The Princess chose her own interiors.

In his diaries, Sir Roy Strong recalled how Princess Margaret's face lit up when she described the house, and

PAGODA CANOPY FOR THE GARDEN OF GOVERNMENT HOUSE

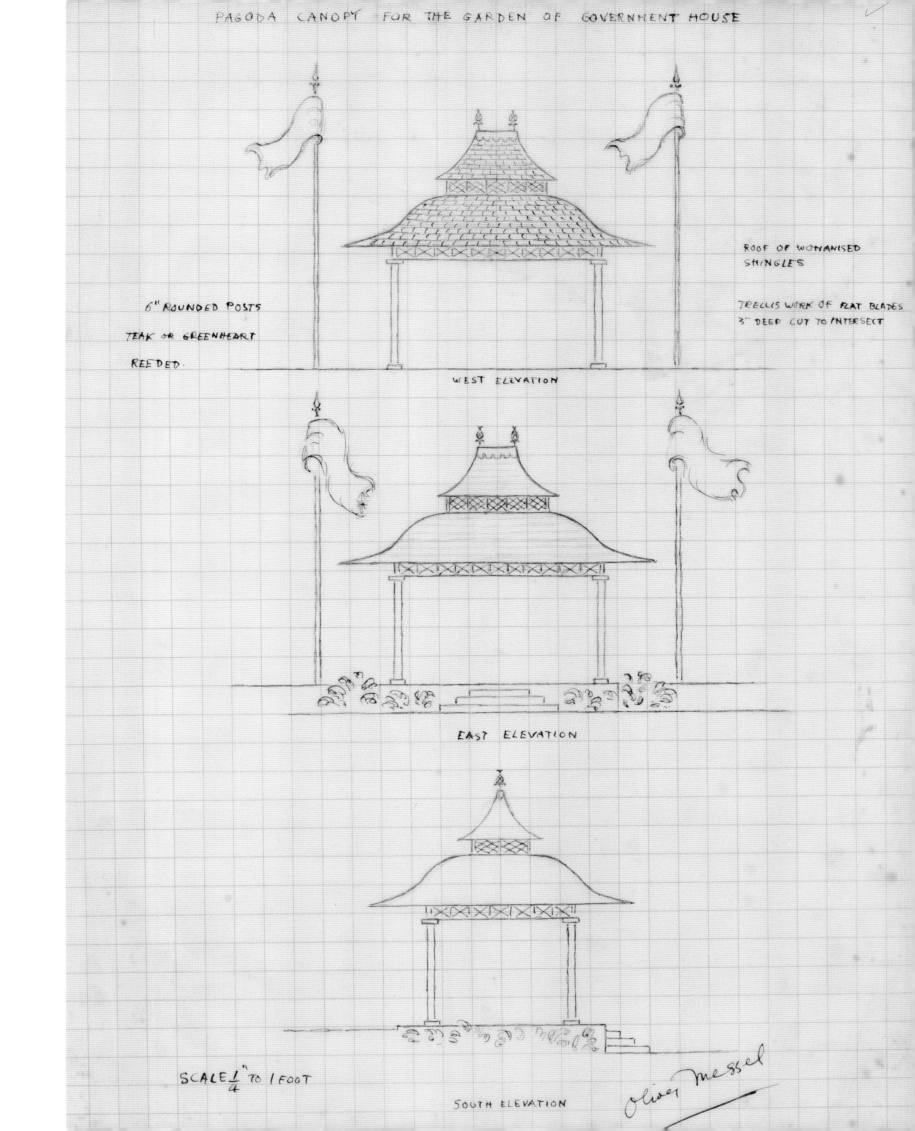

ROOF OF WOTANISED
SHINGLES

6" ROUNDED POSTS

TEAK OR GREENHEART

REEDED.

TRELLIS WORK OF FLAT BLADES
3" DEEP CUT TO INTERSECT

WEST ELEVATION

EAST ELEVATION

SCALE 1/4" TO 1 FOOT

SOUTH ELEVATION

Oliver Messel

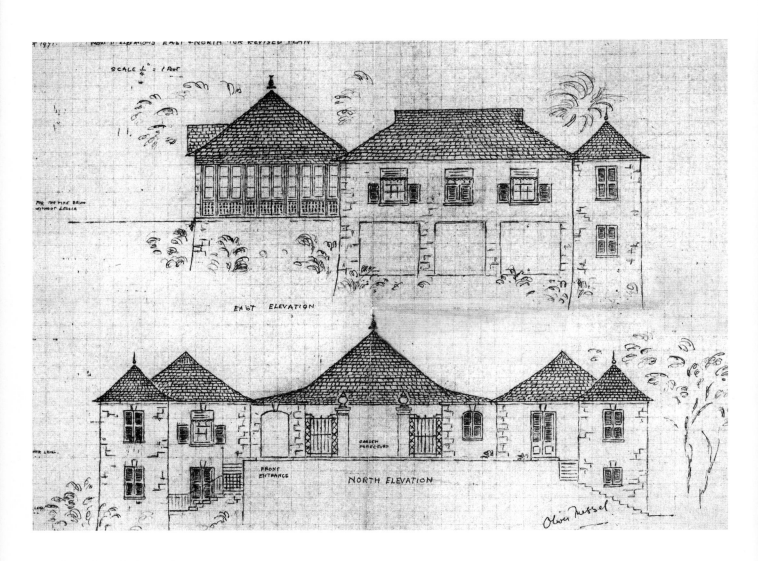

SCALE $\frac{1}{4}'' = 1$ FOOT

EAST ELEVATION

NORTH ELEVATION

FRONT ENTRANCE

Oliver Messel

One of Messel's early designs for an elegant small house on Mustique for Princess Margaret, Les Jolies Eaux, completed in 1971.

RIGHT *The approach to Les Jolies Eaux entices the visitor toward the openness of the architecture and the view to the Caribbean beyond. The house, on an elevated site, has since been sympathetically extended by its current owners.*

PREVIOUS PAGES
*View of Les Jolies Eaux's
seaside facade.*

RIGHT *The main living room
at Les Jolies Eaux, which looks
towards the sea with the view
framed in a typical Messelian
arch, photographed in 1979.*

how pleased she was with Messel's design, not actually completed until 1971. In Charles Castle's book, she is quoted as saying: "I'm very pleased with what Oliver did for Les Jolies Eaux. This is my house, the only square inch in the world I own, and Oliver was a major contributor to it." The house survives, and has been sympathetically extended in the same style by the present owners who have retained the original rooms at the core.[30]

Messel's role on Mustique became much more wide-ranging. He helped with initial trial designs for small houses and villa-type designs in a simple Caribbean style. In 1969 and 1970, he successfully remodeled an old cotton barn into the Cotton House Hotel, and then embarked on a long string of commissions for new houses. Messel made each house quite different, although they shared certain characteristic touches. On Barbados, an English colony from 1625 until it became an independent state in 1966, he followed the classical Georgian exemplars of the older plantation houses, while on Mustique, by his own admission, he paid attention to the French colonial tradition (and visited Haiti for inspiration) and, in the absence of much surviving indigenous architecture, he drew generally from West Indian examples.[31] According to Lord Glenconner, "Oliver appreciated scale; he got the rhythm, scale and taste right for Mustique at the end of 1969. At that time people weren't prepared to spend money here, and it was sheer luck that Princess Margaret came in at that point. No architect would have been prepared to give up his practice to take on the Mustique commitment."[32]

The glamour of royalty and the social connections and reputation Messel enjoyed as a designer associated with Covent Garden and the world of film all came together well for Glenconner's project to create an elite holiday paradise on the island, which still numbers only a hundred or so houses. For practical reasons, Messel was asked to collaborate with a Swedish builder based on the island, Arne Hasselquist, for the construction of the houses.[33] Some of the earliest houses on the island designed by Messel were those begun about 1970 and 1971, on plots that lead up from the Cotton House Hotel.[34] One was for Serge Coutinot, part stone and part weatherboarded, with a little tower looking

Phibblestown, the first of two cottage-like beach houses built by Messel for Lady Honor Svedjar on Mustique, completed in 1972.

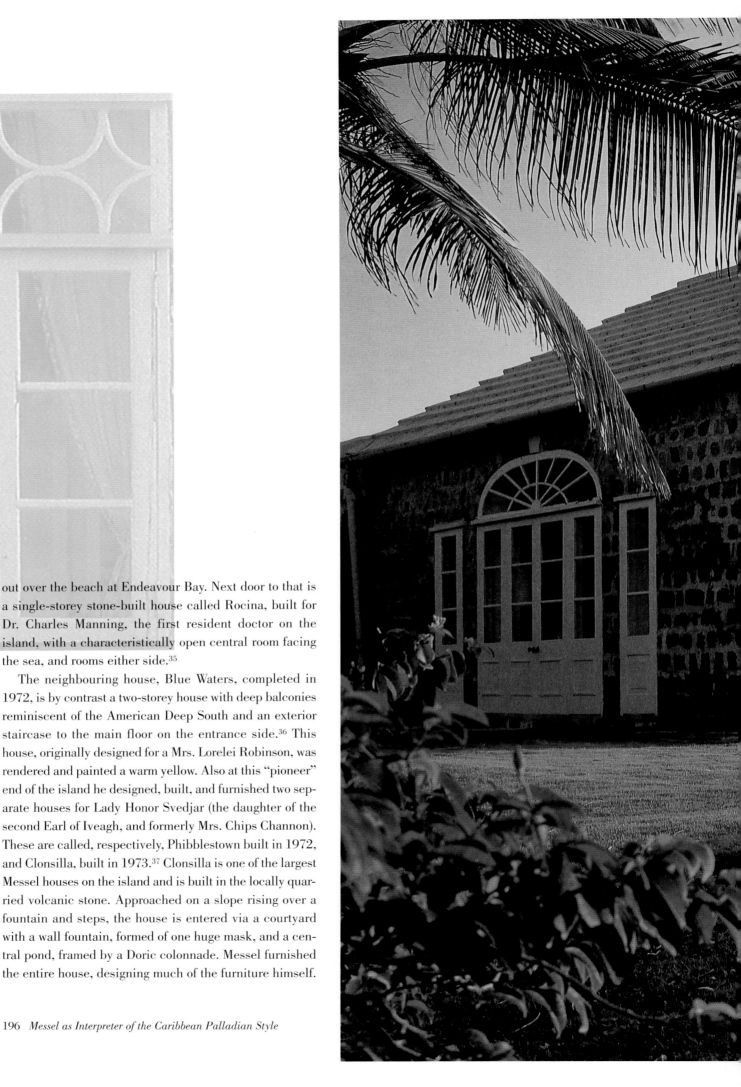

RIGHT *Clonsilla, the second house built for Lady Honor Svedjar, completed 1973, and the largest single house designed by Messel on Mustique.*

FOLLOWING PAGES
The drawing room at Clonsilla, looking through toward the dining loggia. Messel designed much of the furniture in the house, including the faceted mirrors, lamps, and dining and side tables.

out over the beach at Endeavour Bay. Next door to that is a single-storey stone-built house called Rocina, built for Dr. Charles Manning, the first resident doctor on the island, with a characteristically open central room facing the sea, and rooms either side.[35]

The neighbouring house, Blue Waters, completed in 1972, is by contrast a two-storey house with deep balconies reminiscent of the American Deep South and an exterior staircase to the main floor on the entrance side.[36] This house, originally designed for a Mrs. Lorelei Robinson, was rendered and painted a warm yellow. Also at this "pioneer" end of the island he designed, built, and furnished two separate houses for Lady Honor Svedjar (the daughter of the second Earl of Iveagh, and formerly Mrs. Chips Channon). These are called, respectively, Phibblestown built in 1972, and Clonsilla, built in 1973.[37] Clonsilla is one of the largest Messel houses on the island and is built in the locally quarried volcanic stone. Approached on a slope rising over a fountain and steps, the house is entered via a courtyard with a wall fountain, formed of one huge mask, and a central pond, framed by a Doric colonnade. Messel furnished the entire house, designing much of the furniture himself.

Messel designed the mask in the fountain courtyard of Clonsilla, which harks back to the masks he made at the Slade that caught the eye of Diaghalev.

RIGHT *View through the exotic fountain courtyard at Clonsilla toward the sea and St. Vincent.*

The dining loggia, with an ironwork dining table designed by Oliver Messel, framed within a sequence of arched openings.

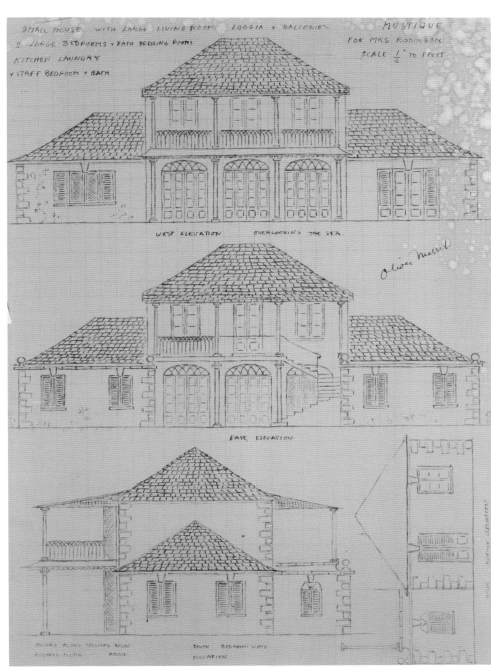

LEFT *Blue Waters, completed in 1972, for Lorelei Robinson, seen from the side.*

ABOVE *Messel's original design for Blue Waters, which has the deep verandahs and classical character of houses in the American South.*

Part of a facade like an opera set, the first floor of Blue Waters is reached by an external staircase.

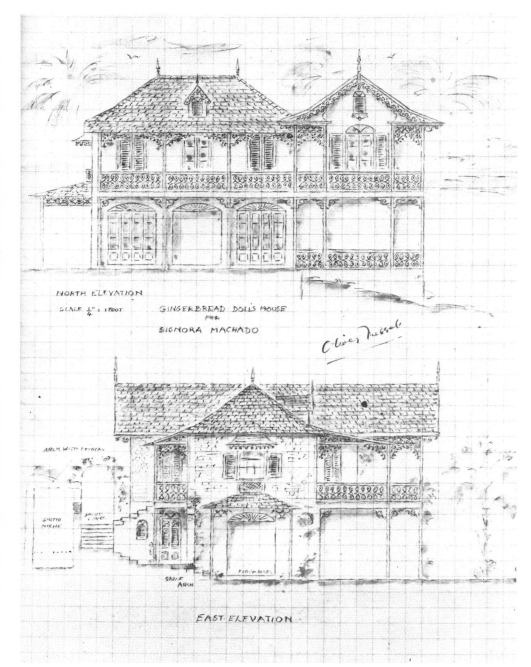

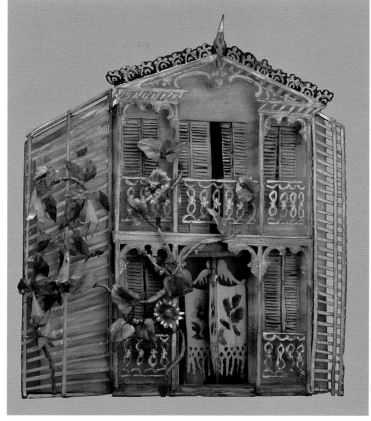

OPPOSITE *Zinnia on Mustique.
Messel designed the original
Machado house on this site in
his trademark "Gingerbread"
style; the house was rebuilt in
1998–99 by Princess Josephine
Loewenstein on a larger scale
following the original style.*

*Messel's design for a new house
in what he called the
"Gingerbread" style, a
traditional Caribbean fretwork
style he revived for his work on
Mustique.*

ABOVE RIGHT *A model of Messel's
1954 set design for* House of
Flowers, *a Broadway musical set
in the Caribbean, shows his long
interest in the traditional fretwork
of the buildings of the West
Indies.*

Also along this bay is the house which Messel designed
for the ballerina Nadia Nerina and her husband, Charles
Gordon: a compact and elegant small house, built in volcanic stone, with a prominent gable over the entrance. The
three doors of the entrance lead to the central room, which
looks straight out to the sea — through a dining room set
within a semicircular loggia — toward the panoramic view
of St. Vincent, like a backdrop from grand opera.[38]

In the light of Mustique's association with French colonial architecture, Messel also developed his "Gingerbread"
style, reviving from desuetude a form of decorative fret-

work in wood which had been used throughout the
Caribbean during the nineteenth century. One of these
houses, built for Rory Annesley, is an ingenious open
design built on several levels, taking full advantage of its
hillside side.[39] Perhaps no other commission so completely
met Messel's dream of creating a house "like a bird's nest."

His other Gingerbread house, on a plot on the Endeavour Hills, looking northwards to St. Vincent, was for a
Venezuelan client, Mercedes Machada; Messel described
the project as "a gingerbread dolls' house" on the drawings. (This has since been rebuilt on a much larger scale

BELOW *Marienlyst (now called Samambia) looking through into the dining room loggia, photographed in 1979 by Derry Moore.*

RIGHT *Marienlyst was built into the slope of the Endeavour Hills with a panoramic view. The wooden seat furniture and sideboard were all designed by Messel.*

FOLLOWING PAGES
ABOVE LEFT *Nadiaville (now called Seastar) was built for the ballerina Nadia Nerina as a series of pavilions on the sea shore, with bedroom apartments in separate buildings.*

BELOW LEFT *Messel's original plan for Nadiaville, which shows how much he considered the detail of the social choreography of these select holiday retreats.*

FOLLOWING PAGES
RIGHT *View from the drawing room at Nadiaville through the dining room loggia toward the sea with St. Vincent on the horizon.*

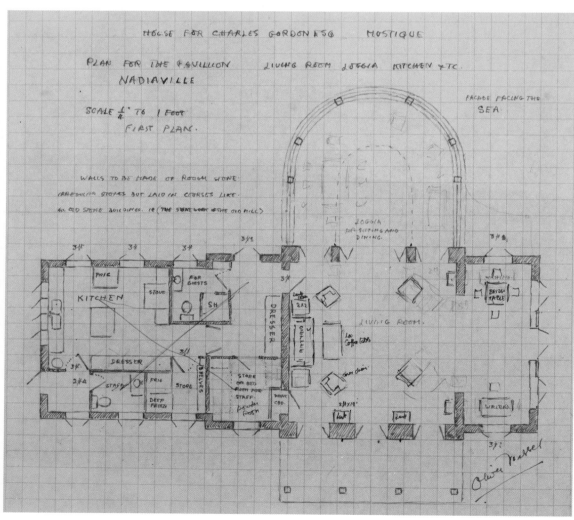

212   *Messel as Interpreter of the Caribbean Palladian Style*

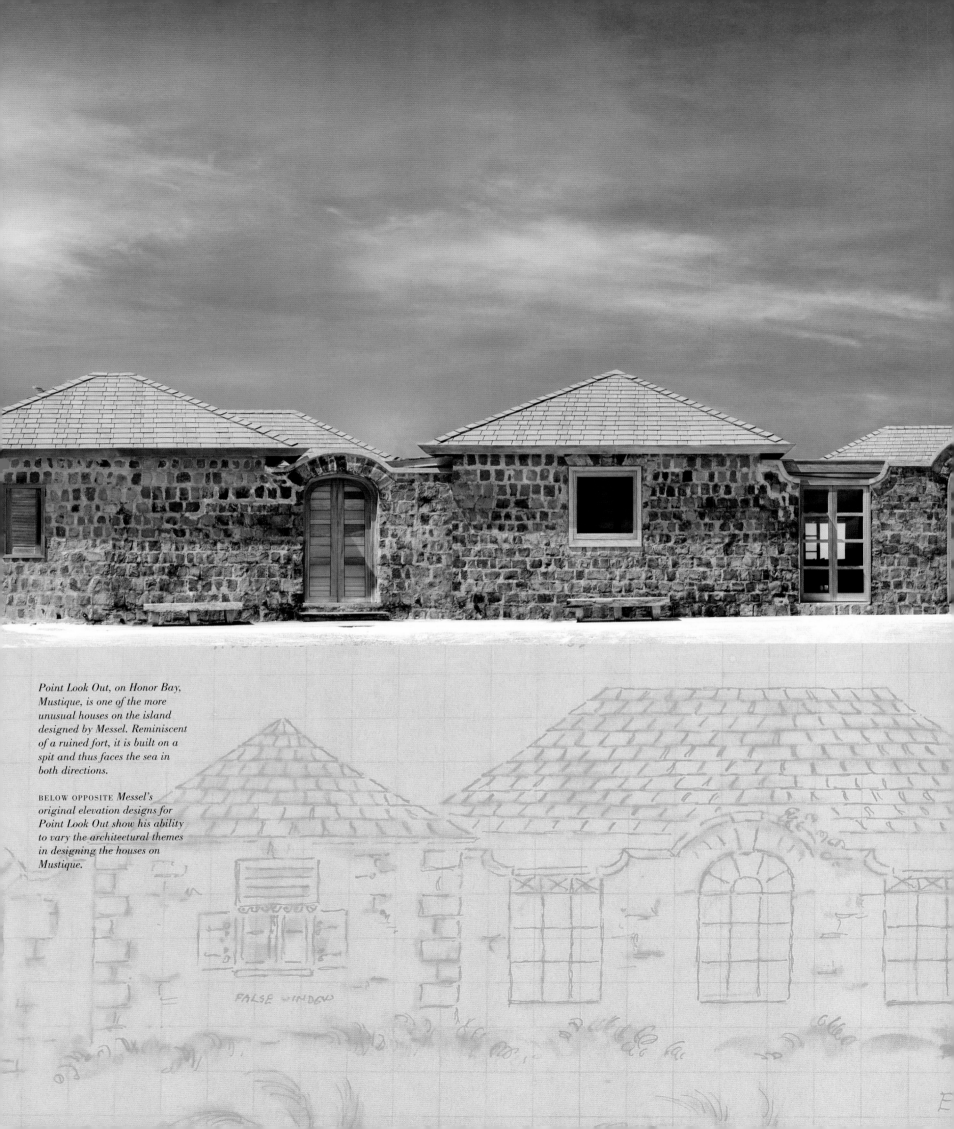

Point Look Out, on Honor Bay, Mustique, is one of the more unusual houses on the island designed by Messel. Reminiscent of a ruined fort, it is built on a spit and thus faces the sea in both directions.

BELOW OPPOSITE *Messel's original elevation designs for Point Look Out show his ability to vary the architectural themes in designing the houses on Mustique.*

FALSE WINDOW

SCALE ¼" = 1 FOOT

ARCHED TOP TO DOORS
ADJUSTABLE WOOD LOUVRES

ALL NATURAL
WOOD

FALSE WINDOW

FLOOR LEVEL

EAST ELEVATION

Oliver Messel

WEST ELEVATION

ELEVATION

FLOOR LEVEL

and in more durable materials, but following the original design and detail).[40]

Another house on the Endeavour Hills was Marienlyst (now Samambia), completed about 1974. It perches on a slope and is entered through a compact, cool fountain courtyard. The main room has a panoramic view toward St. Vincent and is flanked by an open dining area on one side and a master bedroom on the other. Messel was given a free hand with the interiors, and the house still retains a full set of Messel-designed furnishings.[41]

One letter written to a Mr. Baskowitz in 1974, about a project which was apparently never executed, vividly illustrates the care he took in his designs — and how he responded to clients' suggestions. In this case the client wanted a colonnaded pool house like the one that appeared in the film of *The Great Gatsby*, which Messel was trying hard to incorporate.[42] Messel had thought through every facet of the plan: "I placed the living room on the east colonnade wing with a Venetian window facing east to get the most beautiful view but be sheltered from the trade winds, easily controllable as required by push-out windows." He wanted to place a dining room centrally, with windows that could be folded away or closed if needed, and to be accessible from the kitchen, "and not on the windward side to avoid cooking smells . . . This also allows for a garden court with a fountain so dining there [has] a romantic ambience." Messel's account sums up how fully he envisioned the whole aesthetic impact of the domestic space in social, even sensual terms.[43]

Glenconner sold his interest in Mustique in 1977 (although he kept a plot of land to build himself the Turkish-style "Great House," where he had planted trees in anticipation), and Messel took pains to retain a position of influence on future developments, embarking on an ongoing correspondence with Hans Neumann, the new chairman. Neuman professed the greatest admiration for Messel

PREVIOUS PAGES
Messel's tour de force, the Turkish-style Great House for Lord Glenconner, photographed in 1986. It has since been entirely rebuilt but following the style of a domed Turkish pavilion.

LEFT *The carved Indian temple brought from India by Lord Glenconner for the Great House, which was designed for him in a Turkish style by Messel.*

FOLLOWING PAGES
LEFT *A detail of the ornate screen which was used for the walls of the central room of Lord Glenconner's Great House.*

RIGHT *The central interior of the Great House under the dome, with its palm tree columns reminiscent of Nash's work in the Brighton Pavilion.*

and was delighted with the villa at Point Lookout that Messel had designed for him. Newmann said he would recommend Messel to others for private commissions, but he was unwilling to extend any formal status to Messel.[44]

Neuman suggested different designers would give a better chance of variety.[45] Messel, to illustrate the range of his styles, pointed out: "I have designed, for instance, for Madame Machado, a completely different building to yours. She asked for a house in wood, a Gingerbread Doll's House. For the Fuente Brothers in a different position, I am designing small units as a Mediterranean village. For Colin Lord Glenconner in his romantic Palm Grove a 'Turkish Pavilion.' All totally different styles, yet to suit their surroundings."[46]

Glenconner's "Turkish" pavilion, only just then designed in 1978, was completed after Messel's death but was one of the most romantic of the houses he designed on the island; it has since rebuilt, although following the original style used by Messel on the earlier building.[47] Glenconner recalls that they had been working on a chinoiserie design, but Messel suggested Turkish domes as at Hagia Sofia.

Hans Neumann's single-storey house at Point Look Out has perhaps the most dramatic site on the island — set on a strip of land with the beach and the sea on both sides.[48] On the entrance side Messel contrived an extraordinary stone elevation to the south that almost has the character of the ruin of an old fort from an opera set, while inside are a series of open rooms and courtyards formed with Messel's trademark Doric colonnades — all facing the sea.[49]

Other houses built to Oliver's designs were Pelican Beach, a two-storey house next door to Sea Star and Point Lookout, similar to Blue Waters in character, designed for Sir Rodney and Lady Touche; Buttercup, designed for Charles (later Sir Charles) Phillips, with deep verandahs nestling into the hillside; Casa Dalla Valle on a prominent hilltop site; Yellowbird (for Rita Cormack), on a stepped site on the Endeavour Hills; El Seuno (now Grasshopper), a single-storey house on a plot at the base of the Endeav-

our Hills; and Messelia, with its deep balconies on a dramatic hillside site, built in 1979 to designs drawn up by Messel in 1978 for Egas Fuentes.[50]

Forty years later Messel's ingenious open plans, framed in comfortable, traditional, largely classical forms, continue to inspire new work.[51] Messel's contribution to the character of late twentieth-century architecture in Barbados and Mustique is considerable, and his painterly attitude to the relationship of house and landscape, not to mention his skill at making a small house feel like a palace (or part of a palace), were the hallmarks of a highly original designer who deserves more recognition for his architectural work. His intimate, elegant houses are defined by a masterly lightness of touch, an easygoing sensuality, and a quality of handcraftedness. Each one is marked by a carefully considered aesthetic connection with the gardens, the natural landscape, and the blue sea and sky.[52]

OPPOSITE *Rocina, the house built in 1970–71 for Dr. Charles Manning, with Messel's characteristic screens of arches creating vistas within and without.*

ABOVE *View of the Caribbean through the screens of Regency arches which also echo the tradition of tripartite Venetian windows.*

Hamish Bowles

Hamish Bowles is a fashion and design journalist.

When Oliver Messel first turned his protean talents to architecture, on Barbados and Mustique in the 1960s, it was perhaps inevitable that the resulting ensemble of pleasure pavilions created by this master stage and film designer — indulging by turns whimsical Caribbean Regency and pastiche nineteenth-century gingerbread architecture — would reflect his uniquely theatrical vision.

And what visions of enchantment they are. The resort architecture of the twentieth century's great tastemakers and plutocrats had of course long been distinguished by an element of fantasy and make-believe, from the hubristically palatial "cottages" that America's turn-of-the-century robber barons chose to build on the windswept bluffs of Newport to the rambling Hispano-Moresque estates that Marion Syms Wyeth and the dashing showman Addison Mizner concocted for them in Palm Beach after the Great War.

Messel's work, brimming as it is with whimsy and playfully tweaked classicist elements, owes something to the elegant stage-set architecture of John Woolf and Paul Revere Williams, the preeminent exponents of 1930s and 1940s Hollywood Regency; Mott B. Schmidt on the East Coast; David Adler on the shores of Lake Michigan; and to the exquisite Vogue Directoire style of the villas that Maurice Fatio designed on Palm Beach in the 1930s. Messel married the modish symmetry of these practitioners to the liberating notion of indoor-outdoor living that café society had firmly embraced by this period.

Messel's architecture also brought the outside in — his vast unglazed picture windows living up to their name by framing artfully composed junglescapes evocative of Henri Rousseau and azure sea views. And his consummate sense of drama is everywhere in evidence, from the stately entrance gates, which frame a facade as a proscenium arch frames a stage set, to the studiously lit nighttime gardens. This is architecture as theatre, where the house sets the scene and the happy owners and their guests are players.

OPPOSITE *Delicate fretwork on the balusters and columns of Messel's highly original "Gingerbread" style, framing the view of the Caribbean.*

Chapter 6

Messel
at the
Movies

by Keith Lodwick

*Fanned by her handmaidens,
Vivien Leigh as Cleopatra
reclines amidst Messel-designed
décor for director Gabriel
Pascal's 1945 film version of
George Bernard Shaw's* Caesar
and Cleopatra. *Shot in
Technicolor during the austerity
of the Second World War, the film
is a testament to Messel's
resourceful creation of props and
costumes from everyday objects.*

I attempted to use every device to make as much magic as possible.
— Oliver Messel

Costume design by Messel for Douglas Fairbanks as Don Juan in the film The Private Life of Don Juan. *Fairbanks, a pioneer in the Hollywood film industry, and cofounder of United Artists, makes his swan song as the legendary aging lover Don Juan.*

OPPOSITE *The Private Life of Don Juan: (from left) Joan Gardner, Merle Oberon, Douglas Fairbanks, Benita Hume, and, seated, Elsa Lanchester (the future Bride of Frankenstein).*

Oliver Messel made the transition to set and costume design in film as effortlessly as he had done in theatre, interior, and architectural design. He designed eight films throughout his career, each displaying his intrinsic sensibility, his research into period detail, and his creative inventiveness. He was a master of illusion and make-believe: from his early childhood he made model houses, furniture, and painted maquettes, including a chandelier of sticky-paper and fuse-wire, and a dancer's headdress of pipe cleaners. This practical knowledge infused his work and, because he was a perfectionist, proved invaluable to his film career.

The Private Life of Don Juan, 1934
Director: Alexander Korda
Starring: Douglas Fairbanks, Merle Oberon, Benita Hume
Costume Designer: Oliver Messel

Messel's work on the theatrical productions *Helen!* (1932) and Max Reinhardt's *The Miracle* (1932) brought him to the attention of film director and producer Alexander Korda. As founder of London Films and Denham Film Studios, he was a leading figure in the fledgling British film industry and became the first film director to be knighted.

The Private Life of Don Juan starred Douglas Fairbanks and Merle Oberon (who would become Korda's wife).

Set in Seville in 1650, *Don Juan* presented Messel with the design challenge of mixing period detail with his own idiosyncratic style. More than two hundred costumes were designed for the film, and the original estimate for the costume budget was £3,301.14 (around £122,096 today) — more than Korda had spent on the lavish *The Private Life of Henry VIII* a year earlier. Although cuts to the film's budget were made, no expense was spared in making the costumes for the lead roles, a testimony to Douglas Fairbanks's status. It was to be his last film.

Viewed against the simple stage sets by Vincent Korda, Messel's Spanish-inspired costumes are visually striking. The costumes for Fairbanks were designed for an aging lothario: his high-waisted, tight trews have bold geometric stripes leading to a visually stylish bolero-style jacket with playful silver sequin-covered bobbles on the shoulder (a design feature Messel would repeat in *Romeo and Juliet* two years later). Messel's costumes for Benita Hume, Merle Oberon, and the other female actors included the traditional mantillas with lace shawls, wide skirts, and low-cut bodices; they display a light but ornate quality which would become Messel's distinctive style.

The Scarlet Pimpernel, 1934

Director: Alexander Korda
Starring: Leslie Howard, Merle Oberon
Costume Designer: Oliver Messel

Based on the novel by Baroness Emmuska Orczy, this was a romantic adventure set during the French Revolution. Messel's costumes were romantic and playful versions of the period style of dress and represented a trademark he would become known for, in film, theatre, and opera. Now working closely with Merle Oberon, his costumes for her Lady Marguerite Blakeney were daringly low-cut for the mid-1930s but very flattering, and finished off with large picture hats to frame Oberon's exquisite features. Leslie Howard's performance in the dual role as the dandy Sir Percy Blakeney was enhanced by Messel's oversized collars and cuffs, which contrasted with the dashing cloaks he wore as the Pimpernel. The film was a great success, earning half a million pounds on its first release, spawning a number of sequels, and establishing Merle Oberon as Britain's first international film star.

Leslie Howard and Merle Oberon (having her portrait painted) on the set of The Scarlet Pimpernel. *The film was a huge success on its release in 1934 and spawned a series of sequels.*

Romeo and Juliet, 1936

Director: George Cukor
Starring Norma Shearer, Leslie Howard,
   John Barrymore, Basil Rathbone
Artistic Consultant: Oliver Messel

By the mid-1930s, Messel's reputation as Britain's premier set and costume designer brought him to the attention of Hollywood film producer Irving Thalberg. Thalberg (head of production at Metro-Goldwyn-Mayer) was planning a high-profile production for his wife, Norma Shearer, who had been off the screen for a year, having given birth to their second child. In the mid-1930s, MGM was the most successful film studio in the world; its name was synonymous with lavish musicals, sophisticated drawing-room comedies, and high-quality literary adaptations. The studio's roster of actors claimed "more stars than there are in heaven," and the Academy Award–winning Norma Shearer was one of the most popular. The studio already had an in-house team of celebrated designers who had created the MGM "house style." However, director George Cukor wanted to set the film in mid-Renaissance Italy and felt that Messel's film and stage work captured the essence of skilful period design. Messel's arrival at the studio initially caused tension, but in the end he managed a successful collaboration with Cedric Gibbons, head of the MGM art department, and Gilbert Adrian, principal costume for one

ABOVE Romeo and Juliet: *This group of film extras were called the Bellini sisters, their costumes inspired by the paintings of the Renaissance artist whose work Messel studied in detail in preparation for the film. Messel worked with MGM's principal costume designer, Adrian, to design over 1,200 costumes for the MGM film.*

RIGHT *Messel's set model for the Capulet's villa in the MGM motion picture* Romeo and Juliet. *The sets were co-designed with Cedric Gibbons, MGM's resident art director.*

designer at MGM, and he received special credit as artistic consultant on the film.

With a budget of $1,000,000 this was one of the most expensive MGM productions to date. Messel was despatched with a camera crew to Italy where he spent three months recording almost three thousand photos of buildings, squares, balconies, paintings, frescos and drawings. At the Uffizi Gallery in Florence, he studied the paintings of Botticelli, Bellini, Carpaccio, Ghirlandaio, and Piero della Francesca. Many of the costumes and settings were based on paintings of the period. Gozzoli's painting *Procession of the Magi* was used as an inspiration for costumes for the entrance of the Prince of Verona and his entourage at the beginning of the film.

In Los Angeles, the set was designed and built covering five acres of sound stages, including a near reconstruction of Piazza San Zeno in Verona. However, the mix of set designs throughout the film — Messel's romantic vision of the fifteenth-century Italian life versus Gibbons's modern, geometric rooms — creates a disjointed atmosphere. The film is enjoyable for spotting many of Messel's characteristic design motifs that he would use throughout his career. In the Capulets' ball scene, for example, where Romeo first sees Juliet, ornate flowered garlands hang around the high arched walls. The sequence was choreographed by Broadway choreographer Agnes de Mille (niece of Cecil B.

DeMille) and featured thirty choir boys singing a cappella and bearing golden apple trees designed by Messel.

The Capulet garden was designed by landscape architect Florence Yoch (who had created garden designs for *Gone with the Wind* and *How Green Was My Valley*) and occupied 52,000 square feet of sound stage alone.

Romeo and Juliet was completed in 108 days and in terms of costume was one of the most complex operations in MGM's history. There were more than 1,200 costumes produced for the film on which five hundred people worked for two months. Period embroidery was reproduced on costumes which were created from 18,000 yards of silk, satin, velvet, and wool. Fortuny cloth was specially imported from Italy for one cloak worn by Leslie Howard's Romeo. During his stay in Hollywood, Messel discovered Dazian's, a shop in Los Angeles that sold, in his words, "every kind of material ever made." He bought yards of unpatterned fabric, which was then hand-painted and stitched in the MGM workrooms.

Although the film lost money at the box office, it was nominated for Best Picture by the Academy of Motion Picture Arts and Sciences.

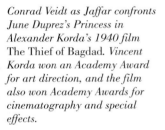

Conrad Veidt as Jaffar confronts June Duprez's Princess in Alexander Korda's 1940 film The Thief of Bagdad. *Vincent Korda won an Academy Award for art direction, and the film also won Academy Awards for cinematography and special effects.*

The Thief of Bagdad, 1940

Director: Ludwig Berger and Michael Powell
Starring: Conrad Veidt, Sabu, June Suprez
Costume Design: Oliver Messel, John Armstrong, Marcel Vertès

In the late 1930s, Messel returned to work for Alexander Korda on his lavish epic *The Thief of Bagdad*, designing costumes for this groundbreaking adventure story alongside John Armstrong and Marcel Vertès. The film was made in Technicolor, which allowed Messel and his collaborators a dazzling colour palette for their rich and sultry costumes. Working again with Vincent Korda (who designed a series of Art Deco–inspired Arabian sets), Messel dressed June Duprez's Princess and her handmaidens in tulle and organza, lightweight fabrics that enhanced the fairy-tale atmosphere. Traditional thobes and turbans for the male characters are in pastel shades, but have strong, deep colours for the film's arch-villain Jaffar, played with spectacular finesse by Conrad Veidt. Despite its troubled production — six directors ultimately were involved — the film was a great success when it was released in December 1940. Its colourful escapism offered audiences a welcome respite from the daily reality of war at a time when both colour film stock and genuine fantasy were a rarity in Britain.

Caesar and Cleopatra, 1945

Director: Gabriel Pascal
Starring: Claude Rains, Vivien Leigh, Stewart Granger,
    Flora Robson
Costume Design, Prop and Interior Decoration: Oliver Messel

Filmed in the UK, towards the end of World War Two, *Caesar and Cleopatra* could have hardly been different to the glamorous Hollywood pictures Messel worked on a decade earlier. It was shot under extremely difficult conditions, beginning on 12 June 1944, six days after the D-Day landings. A flying bomb narrowly missed one of the exterior sets built early on in the shoot.

Gabriel Pascal was the only film director trusted by George Bernard Shaw to film his plays (Pascal had filmed *Pygmalion* in 1938 and *Major Barbara* in 1941). Shaw also took a keen interest in almost every detail of the film's production, from the delivery of lines to the colour of facial hair. Messel was engaged to design costumes, props, and interior decorations that complemented the sets of John Bryan, who had designed *Pygmalion* and *Major Barbara*.

During the Second World War, Messel had been stationed in Norwich as a camouflage officer, and his experience there designing camouflage would be used again in designing this film. Under the conditions of wartime Britain, strict rationing was in place and many costume and prop shops had closed. Therefore, Messel had to apply the "make do and mend" ethos of wartime Britain to the film's design. His talent for creating objects from everyday items and transforming them into something "real" for the screen was unparalleled.

Gauze was not rationed and proved a versatile fabric. Interiors, decorative hangings, and bedspreads were printed in hand-blocked Egyptian and Persian designs or

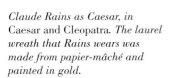

Claude Rains as Caesar, in Caesar and Cleopatra. *The laurel wreath that Rains wears was made from papier-mâché and painted in gold.*

stencilled with authentic patterns of the period in specially mixed dyes. With many skilled dressmakers on war service, Messel had limited assistants, but his close team of makers — Matilda Etches, Elinor Abbey, Maggie Furse, and Beatrice Dawson — worked late into the night sewing replica jewels onto the robes and headdresses for Cleopatra. Many of the costumes were contrived from Indian saris, which could be obtained from the few department stores in London still functioning. Once again Messel weaved his magic, with a choice of fabrics that enhances the atmosphere of a fairy-tale Egyptian court. Messel and his team would create over two thousand costumes for the production.

Headdresses were equally resplendent: materials used on Vivien Leigh's included leather, wax, wire, acetate, glass, beads, and paint. Hugh Skillan, who created these from Messel's designs, also designed and created headdresses for the leading ballerina of the time, Margot Fonteyn.

Work on the props was no less demanding. Authentic-looking antique Egyptian jewellery was created from thin wire, plastic, cellophane, and bits of glass. Gold plates and ornaments were made from a combination of gilded leather and papier-mâché, a material that Messel used again and again throughout his career. For the feathered fans used by Cleopatra's handmaidens in the music room scene, he borrowed some of the large fans from the Messel family home, Nymans, in Sussex (these are now in the Fitzwilliam Museum, Cambridge, United Kingdom).

Shot in Technicolor, Messel's lightweight costumes, diaphanous wall hangings, and rich materials immediately evoke an Egyptian environment, a great achievement given the cold, damp summer that Britain had experienced in 1944 during filming. The final cost of *Caesar and Cleopatra* was £1.3 million, the most costly production at that point in British film history. The film is a testament to Messel's resourcefulness, his ability to work under extraordinarily difficult circumstances, and the skill with which his team of makers and assistants interpreted his designs into objects than could be "read" in cinematic terms.

The Queen of Spades, 1949

Director: Thorold Dickinson
Starring: Anton Walbrook, Edith Evans, Yvonne Mitchell
Set and Costume Designer: Oliver Messel

Set in St. Petersburg, in 1806, *The Queen of Spades* is a supernatural thriller based on a story by Pushkin in which the design and shooting of the picture are fundamental in creating its atmosphere. Filmed at Welwyn Garden City, in cramped and poorly soundproofed studios next to the main railway line, shooting was constantly being interrupted by the noise of passing trains. The film's budget ran out before it was completed and Dickinson and Messel were forced to improvise with sets which were constantly being torn down and replaced with new ones.

Messel's skilful solutions to various design challenges can be seen in every frame, with each prop and period detail researched meticulously, and the same sets having to convey several meanings. The scenes in the palace of old Countess Ranevskaya had to look as if they had remained unchanged for fifty years. The gilded, rococo elaboration of her state apartments had to appear faded under dust and patina. The vaulted hallways and grand staircases within her palace also had to appear sombre with a sense of internal decay, symbolising the countess's pact with the devil. The squalor of the serfs also had to be represented, as did many exteriors, including a bird market and a carriage crossing a bridge, which were all filmed indoors.

Messel's set design and Otto Heller's cinematography complemented each other beautifully, with lighting and camera angles frequently used to disguise the limitations of the space. Point-of-view shots were used to disguise the fact that many sets were either small or half-built, or in some cases nonexistent. Heller used wide-angle lenses to suggest space and width where they did not exist, particu-

larly in a key ballroom scene, where camera trickery was used to deceive the eye. Mirrors are a recurring motif in the film: characters look at themselves at crucial points, and their actions are also frequently seen reflected in mirrors.

The sequence when the young countess visits the Palace of St. Germain is a master class on using suggestion to create terror. A vertiginous high-angle shot of the young countess's arrival at the palace was used because they could not afford to build the palace facade. Heller created the effect by putting up a corner of a wall with a gargoyle on it, directing lights to give the appearance of an open door, and then shooting down onto the carriage. Inside the palace, the camera follows the countess down the cobwebbed corridor until she comes to a huge door, which opens to reveal a gaping black void.

Messel was involved in all aspects of the set design, including the moment when a crucifix is thrown by the old countess onto a glass table, which is shot from underneath to reveal two huge claws painted onto the backdrop.

Fledgling draughtsman Ken Adam (Academy Award–winning production designer for seven James Bond films including *Dr. No* and other cinema classics such as *Dr. Strangelove* and *Chitty Chitty Bang Bang*) recalled, "Messel was a great talent and he taught me a lot about period design. Oliver liked me so he gave me a lot of freehand work to do: engravings of the period and so on. It was a great experience and I learned something about the diversity of a film designer's role."[1]

When the film opened in June 1949, it received universal praise from the critics. Dilys Powell wrote in the *Sunday Times*: "*The Queen of Spades* is something rare in this country, a successful essay in romantic period. Oliver Messel's setting and costumes are among the most beautiful I can remember seeing on the English screen."

At the end of 1950 the Royal Opera House in London presented its first-ever production of Tchaikovsky's opera of *The Queen of Spades*, directed by Michael Benthall, with Messel as designer. For the most significant scene, when the old countess dies, Messel created a masterly theatrical device, placing her in a giant armchair creating the illusion of her shrunken image.

In the gambling house, Anton Walbrook as Herman yearns to discover the secret of winning the game of faro. Messel's claustrophobic interior designs enhance every frame of The Queen of Spades.

The extraordinary baroque lift in which Katharine Hepburn descends for her first entrance was created with John Claridge, who assisted Messel on many projects including the Dorchester Hotel suite created in 1953. Montgomery Clift stands in the foreground.

Suddenly, Last Summer, 1959

Director: Joseph L. Mankiewicz
Starring: Katharine Hepburn, Elizabeth Taylor,
  Montgomery Clift
Set Designer: Oliver Messel

Filmed in Shepperton Studios, near London, Messel's last film was the screen adaptation of Tennessee Williams's play starring Katharine Hepburn, Elizabeth Taylor, and Montgomery Clift. Its evocative settings are arguably some of his best work, including the famous garden set, reminiscent in style of his theatrical settings for *The Little Hut*, *Ring Round the Moon*, *Under the Sycamore Tree*, and *The House of Flowers*.

Messel's research into capturing the atmosphere of New Orleans's French Quarter was extensive as always. He concentrated on images of buildings, balconies, squares, gates, and, for Mrs. Venable's extraordinary garden, photographs of prehistoric forests and plants. Messel once again engaged Hugh Skillan to assist him on the film making the insect-eating plants and outsized exotic foliage. Messel made huge banana leaves with waxed crinkle paper and then mixed them with real plants. He also made vines from paper twisted around in coils and then covered with pale green flock. Over seventy varieties of plants were used on the set and mixed with a painted backdrop and the occasional folly and temple placed as strategic backdrops. The effect was of civilization trying to invade into the monstrous landscape. The extraordinary elevator in which Mrs. Venable (Katharine Hepburn) descends for her first entrance

was designed and built with John Claridge, who assisted Messel on many projects including the Dorchester Hotel suite created in 1953. The elevator is framed by four elegant palm trees and is enclosed inside a baroque lattice.

Messel contrasted the heightened reality of his Deep South house and garden with conventional designs for corridors and rooms at the hospital holding Taylor's character. Sebastian Venable's studio is playfully dressed with masks made by Messel for his 1920s revues for C. B. Cochran.

Suddenly, Last Summer, after garnering Messel an Academy Award nomination for set and costumes design, would be his last film. His successful working relationship with Elizabeth Taylor led Twentieth Century Fox to commission him to design her costumes and wigs for their forthcoming mammoth production of *Cleopatra*, but when the production moved from London to Rome, Messel was replaced on the production by Irene Sharaff (who would win an Academy Award for her work).

Messel's creative ingenuity was evident throughout his career in whatever medium he chose to work. Unlike some of his contemporary theatre designers, Messel was able to also thrive in film. Today, the availability of his film work on DVD — including rare footage of his costume and set designs for *The Marriage of Figaro* at Glyndebourne featured in the film *On Such a Night* — gives us new insight and a tantalising glimpse into the working practices and techniques of one of Britain's most talented and accomplished designers.

Filmography

1934 *The Private Life of Don Juan* (costumes)
1934 *The Scarlet Pimpernel* (costumes)
1936 *Romeo and Juliet* (costumes co-designed with Adrian,
    sets co-designed with Cedric Gibbons, special credit
    as artistic consultant)
1940 *The Thief of Bagdad* (costumes co-designed
    with John Armstrong and Marcel Vertes)
1945 *Caesar and Cleopatra* (costumes, props, and interior
    decoration)
1946 *Carnival* (costumes for ballet sequence)
1949 *The Queen of Spades* (set and costumes)
1959 *Suddenly, Last Summer* (set and costumes)

Film-Related Bibliography

Castle, Charles, *Oliver Messel: A Biography*. London:
Thames and Hudson, 1983.

Deans, Marjorie, *Meeting at the Sphinx, Gabriel Pascal's
    Production of Bernard Shaw's* Caesar and Cleopatra.
    London: Macdonald & Co., 1946.

Frayling, Christopher, *Ken Adam: The Art of Production
    Design*. London: Faber and Faber, 2005.

Geist, Kenneth L., *Pictures Will Talk: The Life and Films
    of Joseph L. Mankiewicz*. New York: Charles Scribner's
    Sons, 1978.

Gutner, Howard, *Gowns by Adrian: The MGM Years
    1928–1941*. New York: Harry N. Abrams, 2001.

Lambert, Gavin, *Norma Shearer*. London: Hodder and
    Stoughton, 1990.

Lambert, Gavin, *On Cukor*. New York: Rizzoli, 2000.

Pinkham, Roger, ed., *Oliver Messel: An Exhibition Held
    at the Victoria and Albert Museum*, catalogue to the
    V&A Exhibition. London: V&A Publishing, 1983.

Richards, Jeffrey, *Thorold Dickinson: A Man and His Films*.
    London: Croom Helm Ltd., 1986.

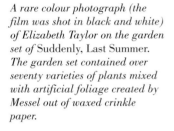

A rare colour photograph (the film was shot in black and white) of Elizabeth Taylor on the garden set of Suddenly, Last Summer. *The garden set contained over seventy varieties of plants mixed with artificial foliage created by Messel out of waxed crinkle paper.*

Sir Kenneth Adam, OBE

Kenneth Adam was an assistant draughtsman on *The Queen of Spades*, and went on to design many of the most iconic films of the 1960s and 1970s, including *Dr. Strangelove*, *Dr. No*, *Goldfinger*, *You Only Live Twice*, *Moonraker*, *Chitty Chitty Bang Bang*, *Barry Lyndon*, and *The Madness of King George*.

The Queen of Spades *was my third film after coming out of the RAF, and I was still only a junior draughtsman. It was made at Welwyn Studios and was my very first costume picture. Oliver was a great talent and he taught me a lot about period design, in this case early-nineteenth-century Russia. Even though I was in such a junior capacity at that time, Oliver liked me and looked after me. He liked my freehand style of drawing. He was a very good painter, but the greatest difficulty was to interpret his paintings and make them work in three dimensions. There were more highly qualified draughtsmen than I to transpose his drawings, and in particular there was a wonderful chief draughtsman called Peter Glazier, who was brilliant at interpreting Oliver's paintings and turning them into technical drawings which could be used for building and decorating the set. Oliver gave me a lot of freehand work to do — engravings on the walls of the main character's apartment, or on his desk, details like that. It was great experience for me, and while working with Oliver Messel I learned something about the diversity of the film designer's role.*

OPPOSITE *Messel wearing the costume he had designed for Douglas Fairbanks in* The Private Life of Don Juan. *This costume is in the V&A Theatre & Performance archive.*

Epilogue

by Anthony Powell

Anthony Powell is a costume designer for stage and screen.

I could not believe my luck when Oliver Messel asked me, at the prompting of Carl Toms, his former assistant and my generous friend, to help him in the daunting project of providing fifty-four outfits for Elizabeth Taylor — and many more for her entourage — in the epic film *Cleopatra*.

Endlessly inventive though Oliver was, any designer will tell you that there are basically only two Egyptian frocks! I remember being with him in his studio around two in the morning, when even he was stumped by the prospect of having to conjure up outfit 53. Rummaging through a trunk filled with exotic fabrics, he produced a length of magnificent purple and silver brocade, which he draped around himself, gazing with half-closed eyes into a large cheval glass, but seeing Elizabeth Taylor.

"Darling Mickey [Sekers] wove this for me," he murmured. "It was my dear father's pall."

Two amusing memories surface from the time spent in the Cleopatra fitting rooms.

The first involves the veteran singer Elizabeth Welch whose scenes as Cleopatra's old nurse were ultimately cut. Delightful, but no longer young, she was still strikingly handsome but *large*.

I was astonished by this svelte hourglass figure she displayed in Oliver's skin-tight costume. It was impossible for her to have been corseted, as one would have seen the whale bones poking through his softly swathed thin silk jersey fabric. The mystery was solved when he broke for lunch. She was peeled out of her cocoon, and I saw that Oliver had taken handfuls of flesh from each side of her body, and ruthlessly stretched them around the centre of her back, where they were strapped together with surgical tape. Amazingly effective but agonisingly uncomfortable, I'd have thought.

Oliver then dashed home to host an elegant luncheon party that he'd arranged to celebrate the recent engagement of his much-loved nephew Antony Armstrong-Jones to Princess Margaret. He had asked the princess if there was anyone else that she would particularly like him to invite, and she immediately replied that she'd always wanted to meet Beatrice Lillie, the comic star of countless revues of the 1920s and 1930s, many of them with Noël Coward and Gertrude Lawrence (now Lady Peel, elderly and semiretired, though still just as funny).

The meal was a triumph, each course enriched with lashings of wine or flambéed in brandy. Unfortunately, no one realised that poor Lady Peel now suffered from alcoholism. As coffee was served, she slid quietly under the table. The staff gently carried her upstairs to the first floor drawing room and laid her on a sofa, still out to the world.

The guests departed and Oliver hurried back to an afternoon fitting with Elizabeth Taylor.

Around four o'clock, the phone rang and a man's voice asked to speak to Mr. Messel. I said that Oliver was unable to come to the phone at that moment, but asked if I could take a message.

"This is South Kensington police station. Tell him that there is a naked woman standing on his balcony, throwing bottles at everyone who goes past . . ."

The 1950s was an era of lavishly contrived parties that few people nowadays could emulate or afford. When the term of office of the American ambassador, Jock Whitney, and his enchanting wife, Betsy, came to an end, they asked Oliver to design for them a farewell ball at the U.S. embassy residence in Regent's Park (Barbara Hutton's old house). I seem to remember that his ideas were inspired

by a celebration given at Versailles for the wedding of Louis XVI and Marie Antoinette.

Part of the décor consisted of fake trees, which he showed me how to make, based on an armature of crumpled chicken wire. He then took long lengths of brown wrapping paper, which he twisted into tightly coiled ropes then carefully half unfolded, and retwisted in the opposite direction (rather like Fortuny pleating). When partly opened out, this gave a convincing impression of the complicated fissures of ancient tree bark, which, loosely wrapped around the chicken wire armature, was coated with a mixture of hot glue size and whiting that, when dry and hard, could then be painted.

No one before or since has been able to calculate so exactly how to create the effect of something to be seen at a distance. What appeared to be exquisitely delicate filigree, jewellery, headdresses, or masks on close inspection

turned out to be constructed boldly (and surprisingly coarsely) out of pipe cleaners and brown sticky paper, often created with his own hands.

Through the windows of the ballroom, he devised a romantic vista of formal seventeenth-century water parterres, like an elaborate knot garden, covering an acre of lawn outside, with a thirty-foot-high topiary work temple in the centre; its candelabra arms of three-foot candles issuing from each column, the foot-high flames reflected in the surrounding dark water.

This magically poetic effect was achieved with extraordinarily economic means. Each parterre consisted of a simple wooden frame, about four inches high, over which a sheet of black plastic was slackly stapled. The frames themselves were covered in the ubiquitous chicken wire, threaded with sprigs of box foliage, which, when clipped, gave a convincing impression of topiary work. When filled

with water, one had no way of knowing, in the darkness of night, just how deep these pools actually were. The temple was based on a tubular steel frame, similarly covered in chicken wire and box foliage. The flames of the painted tubular steel candles were provided by canisters of gas buried underground.

When all was in place, I calculated that the pools could be filled with water in half an hour via a hose pipe from a tap in the garden. It was planned to be the last thing done before the invited guests (which included the entire royal family and most of the upper echelons of the British aristocracy) arrived at eight o'clock.

At seven o'clock, I turned on the tap.

Horrors! The merest trickle of water emerged as I surveyed the acres of sagging black plastic.

The indomitable Mr. Flin (whose firm John Eddington & Co. usually realized the décor for Oliver's party projects)

thought for a moment then said, "Don't worry, it's going to be fine," and went off to make a telephone call. Five minutes later, with a wailing of sirens and a clanking of bells, what seemed like the entire London fire brigade converged on the embassy from all points north, south, east, and west. Money surreptitiously passed hands, and twenty minutes later the embassy grounds had been transformed into an immense vista of formal water gardens.

The papers next day related how a cataclysmic inferno had narrowly been averted at the American embassy, as the Queen and crème de la crème of English society picked their way through the hosepipes and fire engines in the driveway.

Also the next day, we received telegrams of gratitude from Oliver, all of which had clearly been dictated over the telephone. Each one was incomprehensible, in different mystifying ways. Mr. Flin was met on his return home from work by an irate wife, brandishing a telegram and demanding to know the identity of this "Olive Massel" whose "night he had made so absolutely unforgettable."

Oliver was remarkable for his great generosity, giving full credit to anyone working with him for their contribution to any given project. Rather a rare quality, in my experience.

His own house (in fact two conjoined houses) was filled with beautiful and entertainingly original things; after his mother died and he and his sister inherited most of her possessions. In fact, it was like one of his own stage sets in its eclectic mixture of the rare, valuable, and theatrically effective.

What appeared to be scagliola columns turned out to be painted papier-mâché, which didn't quite reach the ceiling, so that if one leaned against them they were liable to wobble and fall over.

The ground-floor drawing room curtains, lavishly draped and swagged, were made of dyed hessian, the folds accentuated by painted shadows (and given convincing highlights by several years' worth of accumulation of dust!).

I was always mystified by the exquisite Rococo overmantel, which, in its central top panel, had an exuberantly scribbled heart drawn in some sort of red pigment, again engrained with the dust of many years. It transpired that when the mirror had been delivered to Oliver's Yeomans Row studio in the early 1930s and was leaning against the wall in the entrance passage, Rex Whistler arrived, and in a spirit of joie de vivre, drew the heart with his companion's lipstick. Several decades later, now installed in Pelham Place, the heart was still there! I am pretty certain that the silvery dust on the curtains and looking glass was not the result of inattentive housekeeping but a carefully cherished aesthetic effect.

For me, though, Oliver's crowning achievement was that Covent Garden production of *The Sleeping Beauty*.

His costume sketches were drawn with charcoal on a pale blue paper, used to give value to white, and shadows were painted with colour made by mixing sepia with a touch of Prussian blue. The sketches were deliberately vague, an impression rather than a statement. In fact, he knew exactly what he wanted but preferred to leave room for manoeuvre at the fitting-room stage, when one is brought face-to-face with the reality of relating fabric to a sometimes recalcitrant body!

One of the most valuable lessons I learnt from Oliver was that the word "no" should be eliminated from one's vocabulary when dealing with artistes, in particular the difficult ones. Say "no" and an iron curtain descends. There is always a way of tactfully achieving one's own vision whilst convincing the actor or singer that you have given them what they demanded too. The classic example was when Oliver was faced with a certain diva at Glyndebourne, who insisted on being dressed in shocking pink, whilst he wanted her to look like the inside of a pearly shell. He made the dress in a searingly violent pink, then at the fitting setting said, "Oh, how right you were to choose this colour — it's magnificent. Now look, we can give it a little mystery by draping this beautiful grey organza over it and then, how romantic it will be, veiled in this mist-coloured silk tulle." As the layers continue to be added, the dress took on the appearance of shimmering mother-of-pearl. Oliver got exactly what he first intended, whilst the singer still felt she was in Schiaparelli pink.

Each time that I saw *The Sleeping Beauty*, I was struck anew by the fact that Tchaikovsky's music and the sets and costumes melted into each other, making an indivisible whole. It became one. Put simply, what the ear heard, the eye saw.

Oliver was a visual poet. He was intensely romantic, but profound knowledge and scholarship (lightly worn) informed everything he did. His sumptuously daring colour sense was allied to the use of strong silhouettes and bold decoration, so that the characters stood visibly out against the dreamy sets painted in thin transparent washes of colour, which receded endlessly into the distance.

In my opinion, Oliver's designs for *The Sleeping Beauty* were his masterpiece, demonstrating everything that he had learned during the course of a uniquely varied career. They have never been surpassed, or, indeed, equalled.

One last, but important, point that I have not so far mentioned is Oliver's delicious sense of fun. As well as being so generous spirited he was endlessly entertaining to work with.

1920–30s	THEATRE	PAINTING AND EXHIBITIONS	INTERIOR DESIGN AND DESIGN	ARCHITECTURE	FILM
1925	Masks for the Muses for *Zéphyr et Flore*. Ballet choreographed by Léonide Massine. Music: Vladimir Dukelsky. Scenery/costumes: Georges Braque. Diaghilev Ballets Russes. Salle Garnier, Monte Carlo, 28 April 1925. In repertory in Paris, London, Berlin, and Barcelona	Exhibition: Masks, Claridge Galleries, London			
1926	*Riverside Nights*. Revue. Mask for "Funeral Dance for the Death of a Rich Aunt." Choreographer: Penelope Spencer. Music: Lord Berners. Lyric Hammersmith, London, 10 April 1926 *Cochran's 1926 Revue*. Masks/costumes for "The Masks." Choreographer: unknown. London Pavilion, 23 April 1926.[1] Preview at the Palace, Manchester, 17 March 1926				
1927	Masks for *The Great God Brown*. Play by Eugene O'Neill. Director: Peter Godfrey. Strand, London, 19 June 1927				
1928	*This Year of Grace!* Revue produced by C. B. Cochran. Book/music/lyrics: Noël Coward. Costumes/scenery for "Lorelei." Masks/costumes for "Dance Little Lady." London Pavilion, 22 March 1928. Preview at the Palace, Manchester, 28 February 1928 *Riverside Nights*. Revue. Masks/costumes for "Nigger Heaven." Choreographer: Penelope Spencer. Arts Theatre Club, 24 June 1928				
1929	*Wake Up and Dream!* Revue produced by C. B. Cochran. Music/lyrics: Cole Porter. Scenery/costumes for "The Wrong Room in the Wrong House," "Wake Up and Dream!," "The Dream," "A Girl in a Shawl: China." Scenery/idol for "What Is This Thing Called Love." London Pavilion, 27 March 1929. Preview at the Palace, Manchester, 5 March 1929				
1930	*Cochran's 1930 Revue*. Scenery/costumes for "Piccadilly, 1830." Choreographer: George Balanchine. Music: Ivor Novello. Scenery/costumes for "Heaven." Choreographer: George Balanchine. Music: Ivor Novello.[2] London Pavilion, 27 March 1930. Preview at the Palace, Manchester, 4 March 1930				

1931

Cochran's 1931 Revue. Scenery/costumes for "Stealing Through." Author: Douglas Byng/Melville Gideon. Choreographer: George Balanchine.

Scenery/costumes for "Scaramouche." Choreographer: George Balanchine. Music: Elsie April. Performed at the London Pavilion, 18 March 1931. Preview at the Palace, Manchester, 18 February 1931

1932

Scenery/costumes for *Helen!* Opéra bouffe by Jacques Offenbach. Book/lyrics: A. P. Herbert. Choreographer: Léonide Massine. Director: Max Reinhardt. Adelphi, London, 30 January 1932

Costumes for *The Miracle*. A "wordless spectacle" by Karl Vollmoeller. Music: Engelbert Humperdinck. Choreographer: Léonide Massine. Director: Max Reinhardt. Lyceum, London, 9 April 1932

Bagatelle Club, Devonshire House, Piccadilly, London.

1933

Scenery for *Mother of Pearl*. Musical by Oscar Straus. Book/lyrics: A. P. Herbert. Director: Cecil King. Gaiety, London, 27 January 1933 and UK tour

Revels in Rhythm. Revue. Music/lyrics: Annette Mills. Masks for "The Strutters." Trocadero, London, 11 November 1933

Exhibition: Designs and Maquettes, Lefevre Gallery, London

Publication: *Stage Designs and Costumes*. Introduction by James Laver (London: John Lane)

1934

Publication: Illustrations for *Lady Sysonby's Cook Book* (New York: G. P. Putnam's Sons)

Costume design for *Private Life of Don Juan*. Director: Alexander Korda (United Artists). Released UK 28 August 1934; USA 30 November 1934

Costume design for *The Scarlet Pimpernel*. Director: Harold Young (United Artists). Released UK 23 December 1934; USA 7 February 1935

1935

Scenery/some costumes for *Glamorous Night*. Musical by Ivor Novello. Lyrics: Christopher Hassall. Director: Leontine Sagan. Drury Lane, London, 2 May 1935

1930–40s

	THEATRE	PAINTING AND EXHIBITIONS	INTERIOR DESIGN AND DESIGN	ARCHITECTURE	FILM
1936	Scenery/costumes for *The Country Wife*. Play by William Wycherley. Director: Tyrone Guthrie. Old Vic, London, 6 October 1936. Henry Miller's Theater, New York, 1 December 1936	Exhibition: Designs for *Romeo and Juliet*, Leicester Galleries, London Publication: *Romeo and Juliet – with Designs by Oliver Messel* (London: Batsford)			Costume design (with Adrian)/set design (with Cedric Gibbons)/artistic consultant for *Romeo and Juliet*. Director: George Cukor (MGM). Released USA 20 August 1936
1937	Scenery/costumes for *Francesca da Rimini*. Ballet choreographed by David Lichine. Music: Tchaikovsky. Col. W. de Basil's Ballets Russes. Royal Opera House, London, 15 June 1937. In repertory on tour to Europe, United States, and Australia. New York 1937; Sydney 1940 Scenery/costumes for *A Midsummer Night's Dream*. Play by William Shakespeare. Director: Tyrone Guthrie. Old Vic, London, 27 December 1937. Revived 1938		San Marco Restaurant, London		
1938		Exhibition: *Paintings by Oliver Messel* (portraits), Leicester Galleries, London Exhibition: *Designs for the Theatre*, Redfern Gallery, London Exhibition: *Paintings and Designs by Oliver Messel*, Carol Carstairs Gallery, New York			
1939			Mural for Wright Ludington, Val Verde, Santa Barbara, California The Georgian Society Ball, Osterley Park		
1940	Scenery/costumes for *The Tempest*. Play by William Shakespeare. Director: George Devine/Marius Goring. Old Vic, London, 29 May 1940 Scenery/costumes/masks for *The Infernal Machine*. Play by Jean Cocteau. Director: Charlotte Frances. Arts Theatre Club, London, 5 September 1940				Costume design (with John Armstrong and Marcel Vertes) for *The Thief of Baghdad*. Director: Michael Powell/Ludwig Berger/Tim Whelan. (London Film Productions). Released USA 5 December 1940; UK 19 December 1940
1940–44	*Served as captain of the Camouflage Corps, Royal Engineers*				

THEATRE	PAINTING AND EXHIBITIONS	INTERIOR DESIGN AND DESIGN	ARCHITECTURE	FILM	1940s

Scenery/costumes for *Comus*. Ballet choreographed by Robert Helpmann. Music: Henry Purcell, arranged by Constant Lambert. Sadler's Wells Ballet.[3] New (now Noël Coward) Theatre, London, 14 January 1942

Restoration and redecoration of Assembly Rooms, Norwich, 1942–44

1942

Big Top. Revue produced by C. B. Cochran. Costumes for "Flamingo." Choreography: Andrée Howard. His Majesty's Theatre, London, 8 May 1942

Scenery/costumes for *The Rivals*. Play by Richard Brinsley Sheridan. Director: William Armstrong/Edith Evans. Criterion Theatre, London, 25 September 1945

Costume design/art direction (with John Bryan) for *Caesar and Cleopatra*. Director: Gabriel Pascal (Gabriel Pascal Productions). Released UK 11 December 1945; USA 6 September 1946

1945

Scenery/costumes for *The Sleeping Beauty*. Ballet choreographed by Marius Petipa. Music: Tchaikovsky. Additional choreography: Ninette de Valois / Frederick Ashton. Sadler's Wells Ballet. Royal Opera House, London, 20 February 1946. Restaged 1952 and 1958. In repertory on tour to Europe and North America; New York 1949, Leningrad and Moscow, 1961. Restaged for the Royal Ballet Touring Company. Grand Theatre, Leeds, 14 September 1959

New proscenium and curtains, Glyndebourne, Sussex

Costume design (with Margaret Furse) for *Carnival*. Director: Stanley Haynes (Two Cities Film). Released UK 2 December 1946

1946

Scenery/costumes for *Die Zauberflöte*. Opera by Mozart. Libretto: Emanuel Schikaneder. Director: Malcolm Baker-Smith. Covent Garden Opera, Royal Opera House, London, 20 March 1947

Exhibition: Designs for *Die Zauberflöte*, Royal Opera House, London

1947

Exhibition: Designs for the film of Pushkin's *The Queen of Spades*, Leicester Galleries, London

Scheme for converting stables into a house at Nymans, Sussex, after 1947 fire, and other suggestions for the remaining wing of the house (not executed)

Working on *Queen of Spades*

1948

	THEATRE	PAINTING AND EXHIBITIONS	INTERIOR DESIGN AND DESIGN	ARCHITECTURE	FILM

1949

Scenery/costumes for *The Lady's Not for Burning*. Play by Christopher Fry. Director: John Gielgud/Esmé Percy. Globe (now Gielgud) Theatre, London, 11 May 1950. Royale Theatre, New York, 1950

Scenery/costumes for *Tough at the Top*. Musical by Vivian Ellis. Book/lyrics: A. P. Herbert. Director: Wendy Toye. Adelphi Theatre, London, 15 July 1949

Costume and set design for *Queen of Spades*. Director: Thorold Dickinson (Associated British). Released UK 16 March 1949; USA 30 June 1949

1950

Scenery/costumes for *Ring Round the Moon*. Play by Jean Anouilh, translated by Christopher Fry. Director: Peter Brook. Globe (now Gielgud) Theatre, London, 26 January 1950. Martin Beck Theatre, New York, 23 November 1950. Folkes Theater, Copenhagen, 1951

Scenery/costumes for *The Little Hut*. Play by André Roussin, translated by Nancy Mitford. Director: Peter Brook. Lyric Theatre, London, 23 August 1950. Coronet Theatre, New York, 7 October 1953

Scenery/ costumes for *Ariadne auf Naxos* (1912 version). Opera by Richard Strauss. Libretto: Hugo von Hofmannsthal. Preceded by *Le Bourgeois Gentilhomme* by Molière. Director: Carl Ebert. Glyndebourne Opera Festival at Edinburgh Festival, King's Theatre, Edinburgh, 20 August 1950. Revived at the Glyndebourne, 1962 1953: Glyndebourne presented the 1916 version of the opera using the same designs. Glyndebourne, 24 June 1953. Revived 1954, 1957, 1958

Scenery/costumes for *The Queen of Spades*. Opera by Tchaikovsky. Libretto: Modest Tchaikovsky after Pushkin. Director: Michael Benthall. Covent Garden Opera, Royal Opera House, London, 21 December 1950. Revived 1951, 1953, 1956, 1961

Decoration of auditorium and Royal Box for Command Performance in honour of President of the French Republic and Madam Auriol, Royal Opera House

Decorations for Lady Marriott's party, Ballroom, Momoville

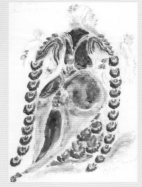

The Sleeping Beauty, part-animated film (unexecuted)

TV: *The Lady's Not for Burning*. BBC Sunday-Night Theatre (BBC). 12 March 1950

THEATRE	PAINTING AND EXHIBITIONS	INTERIOR DESIGN AND DESIGN	ARCHITECTURE	FILM	1950s

1951

Scenery/costumes for *Romeo and Juliet*. Play by William Shakespeare. Director: Peter Glenville. Broadhurst Theatre, New York, 10 March 1951

Scenery/costumes for *Idomeneo*. Opera by Mozart. Libretto: Varesco. Director: Carl Ebert. Glyndebourne, 15 June 1951. Revived 1952, 1953, 1956, 1959, 1964

Exhibition: Designs for a Cochran production, Redfern Galleries, London

Festival of Britain project: supper boxes, stage, and gardens in the style of 18th-century Vauxhall Gardens (unexecuted)

Costume design for Lady Diana Cooper as Cleopatra, Bestigui Ball, Venice

1952

Scenery/costumes for *Under the Sycamore Tree*. Play by Sam Spewack. Director: Peter Glenville. Aldwych Theatre, London, 23 April 1952. Preview at the Streatham Hill Theatre, 14 April 1952

The Sleeping Beauty. Restaged 1946 production ("repainted and remade"). Sadler's Wells Ballet, Royal Opera House, Covent Garden

Scenery/costumes for *La Cenerentola*. Opera by Rossini. Libretto: Ferretti. Director: Carl Ebert. Glyndebourne, 18 June 1952. Revived 1953, 1954, 1956, 1960

Scenery/costumes for *Letter from Paris*. Play by Dodie Smith after Henry James's *The Reverberator*. Director: Peter Glenville. Aldwych Theatre, London, 10 October 1952

Silk scarf commemorating Cresta Silks Ltd.; tie case bearing a rose commemorating the Coronation of Elizabeth II (1953)

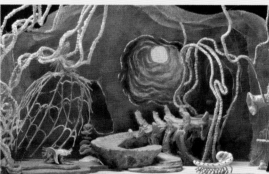

1953

Scenery/costumes for *Homage to the Queen*. Ballet choreographed by Frederick Ashton. Music: Malcolm Arnold. Sadler's Wells Ballet, Royal Opera House, London, 2 June 1953

Silk brocade patterns for Sekers Fabrics, Ltd., the Coronation Collection

Oliver Messel Suite and Penthouse, Dorchester Hotel, London

Decoration of the Dorchester Hotel, London, for Coronation

Programme cover, Glyndebourne Festival

Decoration of the auditorium and Royal Box, Coronation Gala, Royal Opera House

Fabric designs for West Cumberland Silk Mills

	THEATRE	PAINTING AND EXHIBITIONS	INTERIOR DESIGN AND DESIGN	ARCHITECTURE	FILM

1950s

1954

Scenery/costumes for *The Dark Is Light Enough*. Play by Christopher Fry. Director: Peter Brook. Aldwych Theatre, London, 23 February 1954. ANTA, New York, 23 February 1955

Scenery/costumes for *Il Barbiere di Siviglia*. Opera by Rossini. Libretto: Sterbini after Beaumarchais. Director: Carl Ebert. Glyndebourne, 10 June 1954. Revived 1955, 1961

Scenery/costumes for *Le Comte Ory*. Opera by Rossini. Libretto: Scribe and Poirson. Director: Carl Ebert. Glyndebourne at Edinburgh Festival, 22 August 1954. Revived Glyndebourne 1955, 1957, 1958

Scenery/costumes for *House of Flowers*. Musical by Harold Arlen and Truman Capote. Music: Arlen. Book: Capote. Lyrics: Capote/Arlen. Alvin Theatre, New York, 30 December 1954

Justerini & Brooks, wine merchants, Bond Street, London

Suite for the wedding of Sir Berkeley Ormerod, Dorchester Hotel, London

Decoration of Royal Box for the state visit of the king and queen of Sweden, Royal Opera House

1955

Scenery/ costumes for *Zémire et Azor*. Opera by Grétry. Libretto: Marmontel after La Chaussée. Director: Anthony Besch. Bath Festival, 11 May 1955

Scenery/costumes for *Le Nozze di Figaro*. Opera by Mozart. Libretto: Da Ponte after Beaumarchais. Director: Carl Ebert. Glyndebourne, 8 June 1955. Revived 1956, 1958, 1962, 1963, 1965

Arms and the Man, London (unexecuted)

TV: Costumes for *The Sleeping Beauty*. Abridged 1946 production, colour transmission (NBC). Performed by Sadler's Wells Ballet

1956

Scenery/costumes for *Die Entführung aus dem Serail*. Opera by Mozart. Libretto: Bretzner. Director: Peter Ebert. Glyndebourne, 10 June 1956. Revived 1957, 1961

Scenery/costumes for *Die Zauberflöte*. Opera by Mozart. Libretto: Emanuel Schikaneder after Wieland. Director: Carl Ebert. Glyndebourne, 19 July 1956. Revived 1957, 1960⁴

Doll's house for International Paints, Ltd., advertising campaign in *House and Garden*, May 1956

Pompeiian-themed Pavilions Room, Dorchester Hotel, London

TV: *The Sleeping Beauty* Act III (BBC). 29 April 1956

On Such a Night. Includes extract of the 1955 Glyndebourne production *Le Nozze di Figaro*. Director: Anthony Asquith/ J Arthur Rank. Released UK February 1956

THEATRE	PAINTING AND EXHIBITIONS	INTERIOR DESIGN AND DESIGN	ARCHITECTURE	FILM	**1950s**

1957

Exhibition: Designs for *A Midsummer Night's Dream*

Publication: Illustrations for *A Midsummer Night's Dream* (Folio Society)

Exhibition: Designs for *Homage to the Queen*, Brussels

Publication: Illustrations for *Delightful Food* by Marjorie Salter and Adrienne Allen (London: Sidgwick and Jackson)

Boardroom for L. Messel & Co., 31 Throgmorton Street, London

Mural for Mr. and Mrs. Edgar Ivens, Fairlawn

Designs for reconstruction of *Reader's Digest* Building, 216 boulevard St.-Germain, Paris

Mural for Billy Wallace

1958

Scenery/costumes for *Breath of Spring*. Play by Peter Coke. Director: Alan Davis. Cambridge Theatre, London, 26 March 1958

Scenery/costumes for *The School for Scandal*. Play by Richard Brinsley Sheridan. Director: Sam Besekow. Det Ny Theatre, Copenhagen, 19 September 1958

Scenery/costumes for *Samson*. Oratorio by Handel. Libretto: Newburgh Hamilton after Milton. Director: Hubert Graf. Covent Garden Opera at Leeds Centenary Music Festival, 14 October 1958. Royal Opera House, London, 15 November 1958

1959

Scenery/costumes for *Rashomon*. Play by Faye and Michael Kanin, after Akira Kurosawa's film of same name. Director: Peter Glenville. Music Box, New York, 27 January 1959. Previews on tour included Philadelphia

Scenery/costumes for *Der Rosenkavalier*. Opera by Richard Strauss. Libretto: Hugo von Hofmannsthal. Director: Carl Ebert. Glyndebourne, 28 May 1959. Revived 1960, 1965

Scenery/costumes for *Le Nozze di Figaro*. Opera by Mozart. Libretto: Da Ponte after Beaumarchais. Director: Cyril Ritchard. Metropolitan Opera, Metropolitan Opera House, New York, 30 October 1959. Restaged Glyndebourne production. Revived 1960, 1962, 1964, 1966, 1967, 1970, 1972

Exhibition: *Paintings for Fabric Design*, Sekers Fabrics, Ltd., London. Nine Messel designs shown

Exhibition: *Paintings and Designs for the Theatre*, Sagittarius Gallery, New York

Rosehill Theatre, Whitehaven, Cumbria

Billy Rose Theatre, New York

Decorations for party given by John Aspinall, London

	THEATRE	PAINTING AND EXHIBITIONS	INTERIOR DESIGN AND DESIGN	ARCHITECTURE	FILM
1959	Scenery/costumes for *The Sleeping Beauty*. Ballet choreographed by Marius Petipa. Music: Tchaikovsky. The Royal Ballet Touring Company, Leeds, 14 September 1959. Restaged 1946 production		Rayne Shoe Shop, Bond Street, London		
1960	Scenery/costumes for *The Sleeping Beauty*. Ballet choreographed by Marius Petipa. Music: Tchaikovsky. The Royal Ballet, Royal Opera House, Covent Garden. Restaged 1946 production 		Ball at residence of American ambassador Mr. Jack Witney, Winfield House, Regents Park, London Interior scheme and architectural reordering of Flaxley Abbey, Westbury, Gloucestershire (1960–73)		Production design/costume design for *Suddenly, Last Summer*. Director: Joseph L. Mankiewicz (Horizon Pictures). Released USA 22 December 1959; UK 1960[5]
1961			Green Street Club, London 1961–63: Interior scheme for the Bath Assembly Rooms, Bath, Somerset		
1962	Scenery/costumes for *Ariadne auf Naxos* (1916 version). Opera by Richard Strauss. Libretto: Hugo von Hofmannsthal. Director: Carl Ebert. Metropolitan Opera, Metropolitan Opera House, New York, 29 December 1962. Revived 1963, 1970. Scenery: 1976, 1979, 1984, 1987[6]	Exhibitions: *Oliver Messel, Paintings*, Ohana Gallery, London	Decorations for Mrs. Sigrist wedding, Dorchester Hotel		*Sleeping Beauty* TV film: Act III, *An Evening with The Royal Ballet*

THEATRE	PAINTING AND EXHIBITIONS	INTERIOR DESIGN AND DESIGN	ARCHITECTURE	FILM	
		Design(s) for Donegal Carpets, Dublin Cutlery designs exist but there is no record of their having been executed	St. James's House for Lord Bernstein, Barbados (unexecuted) Redesign of house and new pavilion for Drue and Jack Heinz, Leamington, Barbados	*Cleopatra*. Involvement in costume designs	**1963**
Scenery/costumes for *Traveller Without Luggage*. Play by Jean Anouilh. Director: Robert Lewis. ANTA Theatre, New York, 18 September 1964 			Maddox (Messel's own house), Barbados		**1964**
Scenery/costumes for *Twang!!* Musical by Lionel Bart. Director: Burt Shevlove.[7] Shaftesbury Theatre, London, 20 December 1965					**1965**
Following a hip operation, Messel goes to live in Barbados					**1966**
		Exhibition: *Theatre Designs by Oliver Messel*, Wright Hepburn Gallery, London	Alan Bay for Sir Peter Moores, Barbados; additional work 1971–72 Crystal Springs house and garden for Jock Cottell (1968), Barbados, and afterward for Mrs. Botsford		**1966**
			Long Gallery decoration completed at Parham Park, West Sussex (first designs drawn up in 1962)		**1967**

1968

Reconstruction of Queens Fort for Mr. and Mrs. Bill Packard, Barbados

Reconstruction and additions to Fustic House, St. Lucy, for Charles and Vivian Graves, Barbados

Remodeling of St. Helena for Sir Roderick Brinkman, Barbados

Mango Bay for Mrs. Sally Aall, Barbados

1969

Gazebo and advice on interior decoration at Government House, Barbados

Gazebo at Benmar House for High Commissioner John Bennett, Barbados

Initial buildings for new development project for the Hon. Colin Tennant (later Lord Glenconner), Mustique

House for Mr. Mark Gilbey to be built at Pont Carib in Dominica (unexecuted)

Cotton House Hotel for the Hon. Colin Tennant, Mustique (1969–70)

Les Jolies Eaux for HRH Princess Margaret, Mustique (1969–70)

1970

Queens Park Theatre complex, Barbados (1970–75)

1972

Phibblestown for Lady Honor Swedja, Mustique (1970–72)

Coutinot House for Mr. Serge Coutinot (part of the Cotton House Hotel), Mustique

Blue Waters for Mrs. Lorelei Robinson, Mustique

Rocina for Dr. Charles Manning, Mustique (designed 1970)

1973

Scenery/costumes for *Gigi*. Musical by Frederick Lowe and Alan J Lerner. Director: Joseph Hardy. San Francisco, 15 May 1973. Tour. Uris, New York, 13 November 1973

Cockade for Mrs. Polly Hayward, Barbados (1973–74)

Clonsilla for the Hon. Mrs. Honor Swedja, Mustique

The Gingerbread House for Rory Annesley, Mustique

Buttercup for Mr. (later Sir) George Phillips, Mustique

1974

Nadiaville (now Sea Star) for Mr. and Mrs. Charles Gordon (the latter the ballerina Nadia Narina), Mustique

Marienlyst (now Samambaia) for Mr. and Mrs. De Strakosh, Mustique

1975

Point Lookout for Mr. Hans Neumann, Mustique

Pelican for Sir Rodney and Lady Touche, Mustique

1976

Scenery/costumes for *The Sleeping Beauty*. Ballet choreographed by Mary Skeaping after Petipa. Music: Tchaikovsky. Performed at the American Ballet Theatre, Metropolitan Opera House, New York, 15 June 1976. Revised 1946 designs

El Sueño (now Grasshopper) for Dr. Len Bevis, Mustique

Casa Dalla Valle for Sgr. Gustav Dalla Valle, Mustique

Cormack House (now Yellowbird) for Mrs. Rita Cormack, Mustique

1977

The Great House (Turkish Pavilion) for Lord Glenconner, Mustique

1978

Camylarde (now Zinnia) for Mrs. Mercedes Machada, Mustique (designed 1975)

Garrison Museum, Barbados (unexecuted)

House for Mr. Mark Gilbey, Île de Gorée, Senegal (unexecuted)

Messelia for Sgr. Egas Fuentes

1983

Exhibition: *Oliver Messel*, Victoria and Albert Museum, London

Notes

1. My Uncle Oliver: A Private View
1. Charles Castle, *Oliver Messel* (London: Thames & Hudson), 24.
2. Oliver Messel, personal communication.
3. Oliver Messel, pers. comm.
4. Oliver Messel, pers. comm.
5. Christopher Hussey, *Country Life* (10 September, 1932), 292.
6. Oliver Messel, pers. comm.
7. Oliver Messel, pers. comm.
8. Oliver Messel, pers. comm.
9. Oliver Messel, pers. comm.
10. Oliver Messel, pers. comm.
11. Oliver Messel, pers. comm.
12. Oliver Messel, in conversation with the author.
13. Lionel Davidson, *Today*, April 30, 1960.
14. Snowdon, interview with Oliver Messel, n.d.

2. Oliver Messel and Friends
1. Anthony Powell, *To Keep the Ball Rolling* (London: Penguin Books, 1983), 51.
2. James Knox, *Robert Byron* (London: John Murray, 2004), 24.
3. Cyril Connolly, *Enemies of Promise* (London: Penguin Books, 1961), 266. See also Jeremy Lewis, *Cyril Connolly: A Life* (London: Pimlico, 1998), 86.
4. Laurence Whistler, *The Laughter and the Urn: The Life of Rex Whistler* (London: Weidenfeld and Nicolson, 1985), 56–57.
5. Lytton Strachey, letter to Roger Senhouse, October 27, 1927. Quoted in Michael Holroyd, *Lytton Strachey* (London: Chatto and Windus, 1994), 590.
6. Quoted in Charles Castle, *Oliver Messel* (London: Thames & Hudson, 1986), 33.
7. James Knox, *Robert Byron* (London: John Murray, 2004), 66.
8. Paula Byrne, *Mad World: Evelyn Waugh and the Secrets of Brideshead* (London: Harper Press, 2009), 196.
9. Ibid., 14.
10. Cecil Beaton, *The Unexpurgated Diaries*, ed. Hugo Vickers (London: Weidenfeld and Nicolson, 2003), 401–2.
11. Castle, op. cit., 6.

3. Messel on Stage
1. Oliver Messel, *Hers*, n.d.
2. C. B. Cochran, quoted in Charles Castle, *Oliver Messel* (London: Thames & Hudson, 1986), 50.
3. James Laver, *Stage Designs and Costumes by Oliver Messel* (London, 1933), 17.
4. C. B. Cochran, interview in *Dress* (n.d.).
5. A. P. Herbert, preface to *I Had Almost Forgotten*, by Charles B. Cochran (London: Hutchinson & Co., 1932), xxiv.
6. Charles Castle, *Oliver Messel*, 64
7. Derek Granger, "Oliver Messel," in Glyndebourne programme (1956).
8. Walter Kerr, *New York Herald Tribune*, quoted in Castle, op. cit., 180.
9. Charles Reid, *Punch* (27 June 1956).
10. *Nymans* (London: The National Trust, n.d.)
11. Annotation by Messel on the original design.
12. Charles Castle, *Oliver Messel*, 149.
13. Oliver Messel, *Tatler* (August 29, 1956).
14. Charles Castle, *Oliver Messel*, 129.
15. GEG, *Dancing Times* (November 1936), 197.
16. Charles B. Cochran, *I Had Almost Forgotten* (London: Hutchinson & Co., 1932), 279.
17. Anon., *Illustrated* (April 5, 1952).
18. Castle, *Oliver Messel*, 186.

4. The Magic of Messel and the Theatre of the Interior
1. Charles Castle, *Oliver Messel* (London: Thames & Hudson, 1986); Roger Pinkham, ed., *Oliver Messel: An Exhibition Held at the Theatre Museum* (London: Victoria and Albert Museum,1983);

Thomas Messel's archives of Oliver Messel's personal papers, afterward TMA; V&A: The Theatre & Performance Archive, Messel Collection; Amy de la Haye, *A Family of Fashion: The Messels; Six Generations of Dress* (2005); Oliver Messel, "A Master of Décor Speaks of His Art," *Tatler & Bystander* 29 (August 1956); D. Pepys-Whiteley, "Messel, Oliver Hilary Samborne (1904–1978)," revised James Hamilton, *Oxford Dictionary of National Biography* (London: Oxford University Press, 2004; 2008), http://www.oxforddnb.com; obituary, *The Times*, 15 July 1978; obituary, *The Telegraph*, 14 July 1978; additional information and advice especially from Thomas Messel, the Earl of Snowdon, Keith Lodwick, Anthony Powell, Timothy Morgan-Owen, Reinaldo Herraras, Nicky Haslam, Hamish Bowles, Peter Rice, and Pat Albeck.
2. Oliver Messel's own brief account of Syrie's life and their friendship, written as a defense of her reputation after Somerset Maugham had written unkindly about her after her death to the horror of many of her loyal friends (TMA): "She had not only the greatest flair for decoration, but in her lifestyle, and gift for entertainment . . . She took immense trouble over setting the scene." And "She had an immense flair for the luxurious romantic setting for a sophisticated glamorous woman," 1–2.
3. James Laver's introduction in Oliver Messel, *Stage Designs and Costumes* (London: John Lane,1933); Philip Hoare, "Maugham, (Gwendolin Maud) Syrie (1879–1955)," *Oxford Dictionary of National Biography* (London: Oxford University Press, 2004; 2008), http://www.oxforddnb.com.
4. Oliver Messel's personal notes (TMA) with information from Thomas Messel; he also supplied theatrical masks for the decoration of the Buscot Park Theatre, which are still in situ there—with thanks to Lord Faringdon and David Freeman, the curator of Buscot Park, for their help in confirming this. Felicity Cory-Wright later on was involved in Fresh Flowers.
5. Berge Aran, *Austin Val Verde: A Montecito Masterpiece* (Glendale, CA: Balcony Press, 2006), 13.
6. Percy Horton, "Mural Paintings in the Private House," *The Studio*, October 1939, 148–55, which also covers works by Rex Whistler for the Angleseys, Mountbattens, and the work of other figures such as Hans Feibusch, John Armstrong, and Roland Pym.
7. Notes made on reverse of photograph by Oliver Messel (TMA).
8. Berge Aran, *Austin Val Verde*, 13.
9. *Architects Journal* XC (20 July 1939): 88–89; also *Country Life* LXXXV (1 July 1939): 698; and Anthea Palmer, "The Changing Face of Osterley in the Twentieth Century," in Tim Knox and Anthea Palmer, eds., *Aspects of Osterley* (presented at the symposium Aspects of Osterley held on 25 September 1998; published High Wycombe: National Trust, 2000), 57–64.
10. There are a number of letters relating to his camouflage work, photographs, and postcards of old buildings filed together among Oliver Messel's own papers (TMA).
11. Andrew Stephenson and Jan King, *A History of the Assembly House, Norwich* (Dereham, UK: Larks Press, 2004), 31–33.
12. Beverley Nichols, *Down the Kitchen Sink* (London: W. H. Allen, 1974), 50–51; 54–55.
13. Sir Roy Strong, "Oliver Messel," in the *Royal Opera House Catalogue 2005/06*; Pinkham, ed., *Oliver Messel*, 7; Castle, *Oliver Messel*, 126–33.
14. Information from Julia Aries, archivist of Glyndebourne, June 2010.
15. V&A: The Theatre & Performance Archive, Messel Collection, Box 76: designs for arches, walks, stages, dance halls, and performance stages.
16. Suzanne Waters, "In Search of Sir Gerald Barry: The Man Behind the Festival of Britain," in E. Harwood, A. Powers, S. Wartnaby, eds., *The Festival of Britain* (London: Paul Holberton Publishing, 2001), 39–44; V&A: The Theatre & Per-

formance Archive, Messel Collection, Box 76: numerous designs and plans, possibly from 1951, with annotations, including on one drawing: "Pavilion like Old Vauxhall."
17. V&A: The Theatre & Performance Archive, Messel Collection, Box 76: designs possibly from 1951, inscribed with instructions in Messel's handwriting, e.g., "Architectural Features Made of Light Trellis Skeleton."
18. "Homage to the Queen," *The Times*, 2 June 1953; *The Stage*, 4 June 1953; Richard Buckle's review, *The Observer*, 7 June 1953: from Oliver Messel's album of press cuttings (TMA); Castle, *Oliver Messel*, 168–71.
19. *Illustrated London News*, June 3, 1953; "Tent of Gold for the Queen," News Chronicle, 9 June 1953: from Oliver Messel's album of press cuttings (TMA).
20. "Party Scene," *Vogue*, December 1954; from Oliver Messel's album of press cuttings (TMA): the caption describes "the ballroom, built from the courtyards of three adjoining houses."
21. Information from Oliver Messel's former assistant, the set designer Anthony Powell, interviewed 21 April 2010; Victoria and Albert Museum, Messel Archives, Box 72: designs on tracing paper for structures, curtains, etc.
22. Dorchester Hotel brochure for the new suites and pavilion room, 1956, 29–32 (TMA); V&A: The Theatre & Performance Archive, Messel Collection, Box 75 (TM/321/45/1–44); the other designers included Catharine Bray, Ronald Fleming (he had worked on the Royal Palace in Baghdad for the Regent of Iraq), Eric Giles, and John Siddeley; Castle, *Oliver Messel*, 159–63.
23. From Oliver Messel's album of press cuttings (TMA).
24. Jeremy Musson, "Enter the Magician's Spell," *Country Life* 25 (April 2002): 108–13.
25. The late Johnny Claridge, in conversation with the author in 2002.
26. Musson, *Country Life*, 112; Dorchester Hotel brochure, "The Roof Garden Suites: Oliver Messel Suite; the Pavilion Room," 1956, 15–18.
27. Musson, *Country Life*, 108.
28. "It's on the Cards – that Old Mr J. Wouldn't Know the New Place in Bond-Street," *Daily Express*, 23 August 1954, 3; Castle, *Oliver Messel*, 177, 206, 220.
29. "It's on the Cards," *Daily Express*, 3.
30. Information from Thomas Messel, 2010; Castle, *Oliver Messel*, 184.
31. Joe Blackadder, *Rosehill: The Story of a Theatre 1959–2009* (Carlisle, UK: Bookcase, 2009), 9–19; information from Richard Elder and with gratitude for Mr. Elder's kind welcome to Rosehill in early 2010; letter from Oliver Messel to L. Arnold Weissberger, 8 September 1959 (TMA); Castle, *Oliver Messel*, 200, 209.
32. Blackadder, *Rosehill*, 12–13. Mr. Claridge is said to have suggested the griffon details on the proscenium arch, based on a decorative detail from the Doge's Palace in Venice.
33. "Oliver Messel Designs Broadway's Newest Theatre." *The Theatre*, September 1959 (TMA); V&A: The Theatre & Performance Archive, Messel Collection, boxes 78 and 79; Oliver Messel, letter to L. Arnold Weissberger, 18 August 1959, reveals his irritation with his patron who had rejected his design for a drop curtain as "derivative of Tiepolo." Messel retorted that given the importance of Tiepolo's period for theatre design it should be rather taken as a compliment (TMA).
34. The original brochure, 27 November 1959, "Our New Shop," carries both a celebration by Edward Rayne and an account by Oliver Messel. Rayne refers to giving Messel a free hand: "my only terms of reference were to make it as beautiful as possible"; Castle, *Oliver Messel*, 179–200.
35. Messel provided his own typescript account of the works to be used in the original brochure (TMA); some of the shopfront survives, but the interiors have been tragically lost. A fragment was illustrated as part of the furnishings in the apartment of Hamish Bowles, as illustrated in "Some Like It Haute," *World of Interiors*, October 2009.

36. James Lees-Milne, "Flaxley Abbey, Gloucestershire" (I, II, and III), *Country Life* 5, 12, and 19 (April 1973): 842–45, 908–11, 980–84; and with gratitude to Philip Watkins for allowing me to come and see the interiors of Flaxley Abbey in 2010, and for drawing our attention to designs in the house; there is a large correspondence between Mrs. Phyllis Watkins and Oliver Messel about works at Flaxley (TMA).

37. Lees-Milne, "Flaxley Abbey III," 980–83.

38. Letter to Oliver Messel from Phyllis Watkins, 17 November 1972, 3 (TMA), in which she is seeking information for the *Country Life* articles. She kept rooms at Flaxley where Messel could stay, and in a letter dated 2 August 1973, written on the death of his partner Vagn, she wrote: "You know you can always come here at a moment's notice, your rooms are always ready for you. We'd be happy to have you with us." The late John Cornforth in conversation with the author said Mrs. Watkins "would not change a biscuit tin without Oliver Messel's approval."

39. Oliver Garnett and Patricia Dunlop, *The Assembly Rooms Bath: The Authorised Guide*, n.d., 16–17; V&A: The Theatre & Performance Archive, Messel Collection, Box 73, TM/321/44, Box 74; also Messel's own list of works (TMA), which also refers to the York Assembly Rooms, for which there are files of photographs but no correspondence yet identified. It has not been possible to establish his role there. The Bath Assembly Rooms restoration is also described by John Cornforth, "The Bath Assembly Rooms Restored," *Country Life*, 9 January 1964, 56–59.

40. Mirabel Cecil and David Mlinaric, *Mlinaric on Decorating* (London: Frances Lincoln Publishers, 2008), 54–56, which also refers to the meager budget made available to Messel, of just over £4,000, and his work being "theatrical, imaginative, highly toned and textured," and noting how the colors "were deliberately softened in these schemes."

41. Jayne Kirk, *Parham: An Elizabethan House and Its Restoration* (Gloucestershire, UK: Phillimore & Co., 2009), 131; and information from Richard Pailthorpe and Lady Emma Barnard of Parham; and Veronica Tritton, "Parham and the Clive Pearsons," page 10, a pamphlet reproduced in an article from *The Antique Collector*, July 1987. "During the two years that this took, Oliver went to live permanently in Barbados and so never saw the work completed."

42. Letter to Oliver Messel from Veronica Tritton, dated December 1967 (TMA).

43. An account of life in Oliver Messel's long-term home at Pelham Place is given in Castle, *Oliver Messel*, 166, 168; also information from Thomas Messel, Lord Snowdon, and Anthony Powell.

44. Account in *Today* magazine, from Oliver Messel's album of press cuttings (TMA).

45. *Vogue*, October 15, 1963. His dining room is in contrast with a strikingly modern interior with abstract paintings.

46. Osbert Lancaster, *Here, of All Places* (London: John Murray Publishers, Ltd., 1960), 162–63; also see "Curzon Street Baroque," 132–33, in which one can also discern some elements which reflect Messel's interior style: "Once the war was over, however, it became obvious that the democracy for which we had striven was neither so safe nor so agreeable as many people had optimistically assumed, the aristocratic qualities, which eighteenth century culture has so successfully embodied, soon regained their old appeal."

5. Messel as Interpreter of the Caribbean Palladian Style

1. Charles Castle, *Oliver Messel* (London: Thames & Hudson, 1986), 220–60; Roger Pinkham, ed., *Oliver Messel: An Exhibition Held at the Theatre Museum* (London: Victoria and Albert Museum, 1983), 46–54, 66–68; Roger Vaughan, *Mustique* (Arne Hasselqvist & Alfred, 1994); Henry Fraser, *Historic Houses of Barbados* (Barbados: Barbados National Trust, 1986); Keith Miller, *Architecture and Design in Barbados* (Barbados: Wordsmith International, 2001); David Button. Patrick Leigh Fermor, *The Traveller's Tree: A Journey through the Caribbean* (New York: Harper and Brothers, 1950); Charles Graves, *Fourteen Islands in the Sun* (London: Leslie Frewin, 1965), 95–115; "Mr. Barbôdos: Oliver Messel, a Retrospective Study," *Cote de Texas* (blog), 11 February 2009, http://cotedetexas.blogspot.com/2009/02/mr-barbados-oliver-messel-retrospective.html; David Pryce-Jones, "Architectural Digest Visits Princess Margaret," *Architectural Digest* 36 (October 1979), 112–119; David Pryce-Jones, "Mango Bay: A House of Tropical Allure in Barbados," *Architectural Digest* 38 (May 1981), 98–103; David Pryce-Jones, "An Instructed Sophistication on the Island of Mustique," *Architectural Digest* 38 (November 1981), 116–19; Victoria and Albert Museum, Messel Archives, Box 82: a series of architectural designs relating to projects in the West Indies, see the V&A Theatre & Performance Archive, Messel Collection catalogue; also information and help with access to houses designed by Messel, from Nick Parravicino, Robert Thompson, William and Usha Gordon, Sam Mahon, Tony Troulan, David Whelan, Margaret Leakey, Patricia Forde, Lord Glenconner, the Hon. Brian Alexander, Jeannette Cadet, Larry Warren, Pippa Williamson, Mr. Straker, and Debbie Charles; I am exceptionally grateful to William and Usha Gordon, for their kind hospitality at Fustic House, and the Mustique Land Company and Joan Carlisle-Irving, owner of Sea Star, for their hospitality on the island and kindness and the opportunity to stay at Sea Star. There is correspondence about houses in Venezuela (TMA) but I have not been able to confirm whether the houses were executed to his designs, these for clients such as Felix d'Ambrosio. There is also evidence of two projects commissioned by Mark Gilbey, one for Pont Carib in Dominica, and another at Gorée, off the Senegalese coast. I am deeply grateful to Thomas Messel for access to the large files of correspondence, which have not been inspected before to any great extent; as with the previous chapter, I have made good use of all these references but am conscious of the need for the material about Barbados and Mustique to be fully catalogued, which process might reveal yet more insight.

2. Information from Thomas Messel, 2009 and 2010.

3. Castle, *Oliver Messel*, 220–22; Fraser, *Architecture and Design*, 126–33; Graves, *Fourteen Islands in the Sun*, 101–3, 108–10.

4. Letter from Sidney Bernstein to Oliver Messel asking him not to discuss the plans publicly, undated: "Now Oliver—most friendly like—I have to report that I was much taken aback last week when Woodrow Wyatt at Blackpool, in front of a number of people, said he had seen 'my house'. Surprise for me. Then he explained he had seen the model etc, etc, etc. I know it may be difficult but is it impossible for the model to be put out of bounds to visitors at large . . . I don't want it publicised or mentioned in gossip columns, café society or picture books." (TMA); see also Denis Forman, *Persona Granada: Some Memories of Sidney Bernstein and the Early Days of Independent Television* (London: Andre Deutsch, 1997).

5. Castle, *Oliver Messel*, 227; Miller, *Architecture and Design*, 88–97. Robert Thompson in June 2010 recalled, in an interview with the author, the falling out with Drue Heinz based on his treatment of a pair of painted antique Venetian doors, which Messel decided to "antique" by dragging in chains under the sea. According to Mr. Thompson, Heinz was furious and terminated the contract.

6. "Oliver Messel's Full New Life in Barbados," *House and Garden*, June 1971, 60–63; additional information from Thomas Messel, Lord Snowdon, and Nick Parravicino, June 2010, and interview by the author of Mavis Walters, a former cook at Maddox, 16 June 2010; Messel's household is discussed in detail in Castle, *Oliver Messel*, 248–57, with interviews with Messel's former staff, including Johnny Johnson; Oliver Messel's own typescript account of Maddox drawn up for the editor of *House and Garden* (TMA); Maddox is also described in Miller, *Architecture and Design*, 154–66.

7. Typescript of interview recorded with Lord Snowdon, undated, 3 (TMA). This includes his observation about Heron Bay, a mixture of admiration but concern about its scale.

8. Typescript of interview with Lord Snowdon, undated, 20–25.

9. Typescript of interview with Lord Snowdon, undated, 33: "I really would like to build a house like a bird's nest, I think." 20.

10. Castle, *Oliver Messel*, 228; additional information from Nick Parravicino, June 2010.

11. Castle, *Oliver Messel*, 237–38.

12. Information from Nick Parravicino, June 2010.

13. V&A: The Theatre & Performance Archive, Messel Collection, Box 82: design for Nadiaville on Mustique.

14. Oliver Messel, typescript account; see note 6 (TMA).

15. Sir Roy Strong, "Oliver Messel," in the *Royal Opera House Catalogue 2005/06*; also author's interview with Sir Roy Strong, January 2010.

16. Information from Nick Parravicino, June 2010; and information from Brian Alexander.

17. Castle, *Oliver Messel*, 248–49.

18. Castle, *Oliver Messel*, 228–229; Graves, *Fourteen Islands in the Sun*, 109: "Crystal Springs is a house rather than a beach-house . . . best described as Caribbean-Palladian in style."

19. Castle, *Oliver Messel*, 228; Nick Parravicino, in June 2010, recalled the original work at Alan Bay as in 1966/67; work continued in the early 1970s, as shown in letters to Oliver Messel from Peter Moores, including one dated 1 February 1971 (TMA) discussing additional improvements.

20. Castle, *Oliver Messel*, 232; I am grateful to Sir Anthony and Lady Bamford for permission to visit both Heron Bay and Queen's Fort. Nick Parravicino dates this work to around 1968. An exhibition catalogue of his designs for *Anthony and Cleopatra* and his architectural designs held in Barbados illustrates one of his designs for Queen's Fort.

21. Miller, *Architecture and Design*, 106–17; information from Nick Parravicino, June 2010; www.fustichouse.com and information from William and Usha Gordon, June 2010, who kindly allowed me to stay at Fustic House in June of 2010 and experience a Messel masterpiece in the flesh, and Jenny Hall, for introducing us.

22. Letter to Oliver Messel from Vivien ("Nina") Graves, 11 June 1968 (TMA): "The plans have arrived and I am absolutely THRILLED with them—bless you for having so many marvellous ideas; I really do think that with its face-lift Fustic will emerge a tearing beauty. If you knew me better you would realise that houses are my passion and that building them or knocking them about is more of an obsession than a hobby with me"; additional information from Jenny Hall and Lucia Graves; Charles Graves was a considerable author, as he and his wife cowrote *Enjoy Life Longer: A Guide to Sixty of the Leading Spas of Europe* (London: Icon Books, Ltd.,1970). He died at Fustic House. Mrs. Graves was the daughter of Mrs. St. George and the painter William Orpen.

23. Interview with Patricia Forde at Fustic House, 16 June 2010; there are a number of letters between Messel and Mrs. Graves on the details of the work, including designs for curtain arrangements and textiles in the house (TMA).

24. Castle, *Oliver Messel*, 228–230; Miller, *Architecture and Design*, 256–67; additional information from Nick Parravicino and Robert Thompson, June 2010. I am grateful to Larry Warren for the opportunity to study the survey plans of the original Messel house, 16 June 2010.

25. Castle, *Oliver Messel*, 230–31.

26. Information from Thomas Messel, 2010.

27. Castle, *Oliver Messel*, 243–44; letters to Oliver Messel from Government House, 24 April 1969, thanking him for his advice on decorations, pictures, and furnishing (TMA); there is a large file of correspondence discussing Messel's

disappointment with this project's failure (TMA); V&A: The Theatre & Performance Archive, Messel Collection, Box 82.

28. Castle, *Oliver Messel*, 232–44; author's interview with Lord Glenconner, 25 June 2010. Letter from Lord Glenconner (then the Hon. Colin Tennant) to Oliver Messel, 2 May 1969: "Everything you touch, that I saw in Barbados, has been such a success I feel you couldn't go wrong in Mustique."

29. Castle, *Oliver Messel*, 233.

30. Sir Roy Strong describing a meeting with the princess on 26 November 1975, in *The Roy Strong Diaries: 1967–87* (London: Weidenfeld and Nicolson, 1997), 158; I am grateful for permission to visit this house and all the houses designed by Messel on Mustique in June 2010, and would like to record my thanks to the Mustique Land Company and the house owners.

31. Information from Lord Glenconner and references in many letters relating to work in Mustique (TMA); they also discuss the style of houses in Mauritius in other letters (letter dated 23 October 1972) (TMA). There is a large correspondence covering many years of work on the Mustique projects (TMA).

32. Castle, *Oliver Messel*, 234.

33. Castle, *Oliver Messel*, 234–35.

34. Castle, *Oliver Messel*, 240; letter from Arne Hasslequist, 19 August 1970, discusses the projects then in hand: "Lady Honor's house, Lorelei's house, Show House, and House for Charles Gordon" (i.e., Phibblestown, Blue Waters, an unknown house, and Nadiaville). Lord Glenconner recalls (25 June 2010) that Blue Waters was the first to be actually completed. There are numerous papers on file in Messel's own papers (TMA), including such things as a detailed list of all furniture supplied to Lady Honor (3 June 1973) and further bills dated July 1973.

35. There are dated plans framed in the house, seen by the author in June 2010. I am grateful to Diana Wilson of Mustique for pointing these out.

36. V&A: The Theatre & Performance Archive, Messel Collection, Box 82: design for Blue Waters. Brian Alexander's letter to Messel, 18 March 1970, remarks that Mrs. Robinson was "ecstatic about the Cotton House," which shows how important this was in catching the imagination of the first clients.

37. Castle, *Oliver Messel*, 242; photographs, designs, and bills dated 1972/73 for furniture among Messel's own papers (TMA). The naming of the bay was confirmed in author's interview with Lord Glenconner, 25 June 2010. Lady Honor's houses were originally built with concrete roofs, which have been replaced. Both are still owned by a family trust.

38. Castle, *Oliver Messel*, 239–40; V&A: The Theatre & Performance Archive, Messel Collection; there are also letters (including 7 March 1974) about the garden and plants that act as wind breaks, such as zoysia grass, sea grapes, and oleanders (TMA). Signed copies of the original plans are framed at the house and were seen by the author in June 2010.

39. David Pryce-Jones, "On Mustique: The Tropical Charm of the Gingerbread House," *Architectural Digest* 37 (July/August 1980), 58–65; Pinkham, ed., *Oliver Messel*, 84: Signora Machado's house design is illustrated here. Designs may have been drawn up earlier but work did not begin before 1978, as a series of letters show (TMA).

40. Now known as Zinnia, the house was rebuilt on a larger scale, following closely the detail and style of the original house as designed by Messel; information from Brian Alexander and Jeannette Cadet.

41. There is a series of letters with Mrs. De Strakosh which reveal that she gave him a considerable free hand in the furnishing of the house, and that much of the original furniture still remains in the house (TMA). Her first letter from the house, dated 24 December 1975: "My first letter written at Marienlyst goes to you, to thank you for all the efforts you have put into it. However they SHOW and our house is a real jewel. We do appreciate all your touches and are happy beyond words."

42. Oliver Messel, letter to Mr. Baskowitz, 17 October 1974, 1 (TMA).

43. Oliver Messel, letter to Mr. Baskowitz, 17 October 1974, 2 (TMA).

44. Hans Neumann, letters to Oliver Messel, 17 August 1977, 1, and 25 April 1978 (TMA); Oliver Messel, letter to Hans Neumann, 29 August 1977, 1 (TMA).

45. Oliver Messel, letter to Hans Neumann, 29 August 1977, 1 (TMA).

46. Information from the Mustique Land Company; author's interview with Lord Glenconner, 25 June 2010.

47. There are plans and elevations for Point Look Out (TMA).

48. I am grateful to Mr. Bryan Adams for permission to visit Point Look Out in June 2010.

49. Vaughan, *Mustique*; letters and plans in Messel's papers include a number from Sir Rodney Touche, Bt., such as 7 February 1975: "Your design for our house is absolutely delightful. Very pleasing and exciting . . . Under no circumstances would we prefer a single-storey house. We very much want two storey and we love the outside staircase" (TMA); information from the Mustique Land Company; information from Tony Milsom of Barbados and owner of Messelia on Mustique, to whom I am grateful for his hospitality and for showing me Messel's signed drawings for this house.

50. There are notes and designs for James Gilbey's house at Ponte Carib, Dominica, which was not executed, among Messel's own papers from 1977/8 (TMA).

51. For instance, in the early days there was Obsidian, discussed with Messel before his death, and built in Messel's Gingerbread style to a design by the Earl of Lichfield; also since 2000, Hibiscus and Coccoloba, on Mustique (see *The Exclusive Villas of Mustique* [2010] and new works by architect Larry Warren of St. Nicholas Abbey, Barbados.

52. Interview with architect Larry Warren of St. Nicholas Abbey, Barbados, 16 June 2010, who has worked on restoration of and extensions to five Messel-designed houses. Mr. Warren spoke of the importance of respecting the quality of Messel's own work and how he admired the similarly respectful nature of Messel's own approach to design.

6. Messel at the Movies

1. Christopher Frayling, *Ken Adam and the Art of Production Design* (London: Faber and Faber, 2005).

Chronology

1. Cochran revues were previewed in Manchester, during which the production and running order were further developed prior to performances in London.

2. The program credits Novello and Beverley Nichols with the duet "Heaven," but it is not clear if they composed the music for the scene, or if it was instead Vivian Ellis, who composed most of the music for the revue.

3. The Sadler's Wells Ballet became the Royal Ballet in 1956.

4. *Die Entführung aus dem Serail* and *Die Zauberflöte* were performed with revivals of *Idomeneo* and *Le Nozze di Figaro* as part of the bicentenary celebrations of Mozart's birth.

5. Katharine Hepburn's costumes were designed by Norman Harnell and Elizabeth Taylor's costumes by Jean Louis.

6. From 1976 on, only Messel's scenery was used. Costumes were designed by Jane Greenwood.

7. Shevlove was brought in after the original director, Joan Littlewood, left the production.

Photography Credits

Angus McBain: 255
Arne Hasselquiste- Mustique: 195, 197, 198–99, 200, 201, 202, 203, 204, 206–7
Berge Aran Val Verde: 93, 87, 89
Bryan Adams: 214–15
Byron Slater, courtesy of William and Usha Gordon: 175, 176–77, 178–79, 180–81, 182–83
Clarence Sinclair Bull: 11
Claude Harris, courtesy of V&A, T&PC: 58
Country Life: 18, 103, 106-7, 108, 110–11, 112, 120
Courtesy of Keith Lodwick Collection: 234–35
Courtesy of the Cecil Beaton Studio Archive at Sothebys: 35, 40–41, 47, 48
Cutting, Fenwick: 27
Dale Curtis: 209: 211
Daniel Christaldi: 160–61
Derry Moore: 109, 144–45, 150, 151, 152–53, 154–55, 157, 162–63, 164, 165, 167, 168–69, 170–71, 173, 189, 190, 193, 210, 216–17, 218, 220, 221, 225
Donald Darroch: 229, 231
Dorchester Hotel, London: 113, 114–15, 138
Earl of Rosse, Birr Castle Collection: 22
Edward Mandinian: 148
Edward Reeves, Lewes: 100
Fitzwilliam Museum, University of Cambridge, UK/Bridgeman Art Library: 15
Foto Giacomelli, Venezia: 39
Frank Sharman, Royal Opera House Covent Garden: 79
George Hurrell: 249
Horst: 23
James De Vries: 31
Jeremy Musson: 158, 159, 212
Jeremy Whitaker: 125
Justerini & Brooks: 132–33
Kobal Collection: 247
Linley Sambourne House, Royal Borough of Kensington and Chelsea: 16–17
Lord Faringdon, Buscot House, National Trust: 91
Mellon Collection; National Gallery of Art, Washington, D.C./Bridgeman Art Library: 21
Mustique Company Archives Ltd.: 186–87, 213, 222, 223
National Trust, Nymans Archives: 12, 19, 20, 28
Nic Barlow: 108, 122–23, 124, 126–27, 128–29, 140–41
Nick McCann, courtesy of Lady Emma Barnard, Parham Park Ltd.: 137
Phil Rigby, Cumbria Life: 135
Planet News: 37
Snowdon: 2–3, 9, 25, 53, 54–55, 68–69, 71, 139, 147, 251
Thomas Messel Archives: 4–5, 13, 34, 38, 42–43, 45, 46, 49, 51, 62, 63, 88, 90, 94, 95, 96, 97, 98, 99, 105, 118–19, 130, 131, 136, 148, 149, 174, 184, 185, 205, 208, 212, 215, 226–27, 233, 252–53
Victoria and Albert Museum, Theatre and Performance Collection: 1, 73, 57, 59, 60–61, 64, 65, 66, 70, 72, 74–75, 76, 77, 78, 80, 81, 82–83, 85, 104, 116, 117, 134, 166, 188, 208, 228, 232, 236, 237, 239, 240, 241, 243, 245
Wysard, Anthony, Reserved; Collection National Portrait Gallery, London: 32–33

Every effort has been made to obtain permission from the relevant copyright holders and to ensure that all credits are correct. We have acted in good faith and on the best information available to us at the time of publication. We apologise for any inadvertent omissions, which will be corrected in future editions if notification is given to the publisher in writing.

Index

First published in the United States of America in 2011 by Rizzoli International Publications, Inc.
300 Park Avenue South, New York, NY 10010
www.rizzoliusa.com

ISBN: 978-0-8478-3396-2
LCCN: 2011932839

© 2011 Rizzoli International Publications, Inc.

Designed by Abigail Sturges

Distributed to the U.S. trade by Random House, New York

Printed and bound in China

2011 2012 2013 2014 2015 / 10 9 8 7 6 5 4 3 2 1